Escape from the Dungeon: Jennifer's Survival Story from the Wrath of Anger, Intimidation and Abuse

by

Jennifer Stephens

www.jenniferstephens.org
wisconsinvision@aol.com
P.O. Box 510562
New Berlin, WI 53151

copyright 2005 Jennifer Stephens

Note for Librarians: A cataloguing record for this book is available from Library
and Archives Canada at www.collectionscanada.ca/amicus/index-e.html

ISBN 1-4120-6579-8

*Printed in Victoria, BC, Canada. Printed on paper with minimum 30% recycled fibre. Trafford's
print shop runs on "green energy" from solar, wind and other environmentally-friendly power
sources.*

TRAFFORD
PUBLISHING™

Offices in Canada, USA, Ireland and UK

This book was published *on-demand* in cooperation with Trafford Publishing.
On-demand publishing is a unique process and service of making a book
available for retail sale to the public taking advantage of on-demand
manufacturing and Internet marketing. On-demand publishing includes
promotions, retail sales, manufacturing, order fulfilment, accounting and
collecting royalties on behalf of the author.

Book sales for North America and international:
Trafford Publishing, 6E–2333 Government St.,
Victoria, BC V8T 4P4 CANADA
phone 250 383 6864 (toll-free 1 888 232 4444)
fax 250 383 6804; email to orders@trafford.com
Book sales in Europe:
Trafford Publishing (UK) Limited, 9 Park End Street, 2nd Floor
Oxford, UK OX1 1HH UNITED KINGDOM
phone 44 (0)1865 722 113 (local rate 0845 230 9601)
facsimile 44 (0)1865 722 868; info.uk@trafford.com
Order online at:
trafford.com/05-1490

10 9 8 7 6 5 4 3 2

This book is dedicated to:

Brad Schimel, Assistant District Attorney, Waukesha County, Wisconsin, for committing to the case to the bitter end. Without Brad, we would not have justice today and mom would continue to ruin her childrens' lives. On behalf of my brothers and sisters and myself, the words thank you could never cover our gratitude.

Detective Ryan Park of the New Berlin Police Department for being so vigilant in his investigation and chasing every lead no matter how small.

My best friend Meg – you have been my friend for life, good, bad and ugly. You never pitied me, you never looked down on me, you were just there and you saved my life in September, 1987. Without you, I would not have had the strength to leave the home, thank you.

Contents

Forward Meg

Numerous statues of various animals cast eerie shadows on the lawn. A van and the family station wagon were usually parked in the driveway. The neighbors claim they had no idea. The small, white mansion-like house was always very quiet...at least on the outside. Jenny was different – certainly not like the average American teen. The second of sixteen children, she never wore make-up, her ears weren't pierced, she didn't go out, she always wore a skirt and her hair was nearly down to her waist. The day Jenny came to school nearly bald, was the day everyone was finally forced to admit something was wrong. Jenny's story is a bad dream come true. A life of beatings, verbal abuse and neglect, and even though she escaped years ago, the latest chapters of the reoccurring dream have yet to find true closure. Dreams are; however, exactly what has made Jenny not a survivor, but an overachiever. A Major in the U.S. army with two Bachelor's Degrees and a MBA to her name and working on a Doctorate in Law, she is a go-getter. Many shake their heads at her "crazy ideas", but then she goes out and proves that hard work and determination are the means to most dreams. Her latest crazy idea is to tell her story. She wants closure to the chapters about abuse. She wants to inspire other abused children and spouses, to create awareness, and to help her siblings, many of whom she just recently met. Jenny called me out of the blue and said she had written a book. I knew better than to smirk. Jenny always does what she dreams.

-Meg

Escape from the Dungeon

Overview from the District Attorney
Brad Schimel

As I reflect on the abuse that went on in the Stephens house for over three decades, it occurs to me that if I wrote a work of fiction that described these events, readers would reject it as too bizarre and horrific to be believable. No one would believe a character like Linda Stephens could continue to get away with such outrageous behavior for so long. And yet, none of this is fiction. Each new group of the 16 children suffered abuse that was hauntingly similar to what their older siblings experienced. It was as if they were on an assembly line; only Linda Stephens was not building anything. Rather, she was trying to destroy her children.

I will never forget the image of Linda Stephens sitting at sentencing in her comically enormous blond wig and silver tiara, acting for the cameras like she had no idea why her children would have such resentment for her. As Judge Dreyfus wisely noted, she was trying to manipulate her children and the justice system right to the end. I will never forget how painful it was for her children to get up one after another and tell her and the court that they have no mother.

Somehow, once each of the Stephens children has escaped their mother's control, they have defied the odds and have thrived. The younger ones are healthy and happy and are exhibiting abilities and aptitudes no one ever thought they possessed. The older siblings have become wonderful, loving parents to their own children and have excelled in every aspect of their lives. They all had an excuse to fail, to abuse alcohol or drugs, and to continue the cycle of abuse that their parents started. It has taken tremendous strength of character and courage for each of them to throw off their twisted and warped upbringing. I am proud of them. It was a privilege to have been able to get to know them and help them close this chapter of their lives.

-Brad Schimel, Assistant District Attorney, Waukesha County, Wisconsin

Chapter 1

Introduction

Jennifer M. Stephens

September 14, 1987 - This is a day I will never forget; it was the day I looked into my mother's eyes and saw my own mortality. It was the day I wanted to give up trying and just pass away to the next world. This day is engrained in so many of the kids' minds. Each child that witnessed it can tell you a story of psychological warfare, utter pain, mental anguish, and overall defeat. This day was worse than anything I have faced in 14 years in the military. This day was worse than anything I could imagine. It was the day my mother tried to kill me and the day I saw the devil in her eyes.

This is a story of psychological terror at the hands of my mother. I am the second oldest of 16 children and the stories I am about to describe relay what it was like to live under the reign of terror of our mother. The abuse started about 35 years ago in 1970. Who knew there would be 16 direct victims and so many other people affected by her manipulations when all was said and done. Hind sight is truly 20/20 and had things been handled differently in the 1987 felony child abuse case in Waukesha County, there wouldn't be this tale to tell today in 2005.

There are two distinct time periods in this story: the 17 years prior to 1987 and the 18 years after 1987. Unfortunately for all of us children involved, the story reads nearly the same with only the children involved changing. You will find parallels in the years before and after 1987 that I still can't believe today. I was part of the situation from the beginning and a catalyst for this coming to light. What you will see is a very large break in the system but above all, the master manipulation that would rival the greatest minds. By manipulating her children, the social workers, the lawyers and the prosecutors, mom got off in 1987 when she was facing 18 counts of felony and misdemeanor child abuse charges, $180,000 in fines and 30 years in prison. Her ability to walk away without a scar only enabled mom and her psychotic manipulating mind to abuse again without fear for the next 18 years. It is heartbreaking to know and live with the fact that, although these actions had been addressed in the past, she ended up inflicting the same thing on my brothers and sisters as soon as the Department of Social Services stepped out of the picture in the late eighties. You often hear that history repeats itself, but I never would have imagined it could be the exact same acts of manipulation, terror and intimidating abuse over such a long period of time.

I changed the names of my brothers and sisters for a variety of reasons, one being that some do not want anything to do with this situation anymore and just want to see it go away and I must protect that privacy. Others have so much on their plates and/or a distinguished career and I would not want to compromise that success. My story here is just one story of 16 and if every child told their story you would have a miniseries in the making. If they choose to, they can say who they are in their own way in their own time. For purposes here the names of the children in age order: Ted, Jennifer (myself), Holly, Elizabeth, Chip, Roger, Ricky, Suzy, Michael, Andie, Lisa, Mary, Jeffery, Nick, Charlie, and Amber.

I have two goals for writing this book - actually three - with the first being a healing process. This story has been 3 ½ decades in the making and I feel this situation can be used to help those in similar situations. I want folks to know that it only takes one vigilant person to make a difference in these cases, and someone reading this may become one of those vigilant people. I am the oldest daughter and have seen this lifelong abuse and manipulation from mom grow in slow times and fast and feel compelled to share this story so that others may find solace and triumph for a similar tragedy they may be facing. The second reason is that I want to be able to give any of the kids who want to go to college the opportunity to go. I am quite confident that an education would have some pretty positive results on the kids. The first step to recovery is self-esteem and receiving an education would help them achieve that possibility. The third and most important reason is justice. As of today, June 2005, I am not fully convinced mom will be held accountable to the level she deserves. I would like at the very least to let people know the woman I have known my entire life and hopefully raise enough awareness so she never has the opportunity to put another child in harm's way. It is my opinion that, even if she is convicted, she will play the martyr and say she is only plea bargaining to spare the feelings of the children and then spend her years in prison plotting a slow and painful revenge against any person who has spoken against her.

The stories here are told from my point of view with input from several public records available in Waukesha County. I chose to use public records and my own personal memories mostly for my own protection and so that I wouldn't have to ask my siblings to endure the memories brought out in a project like this. It is hard to believe sometimes that we actually lived this lifestyle and in all honestly, I find that I block most of it out in my day-to-day workings in life; however, this past year, I have been plagued with haunting memories of the atrocities my mother inflicted onto other people, including her dead parents and her own children, for her own personal gain. I continue to remain appalled at how this woman is able to walk the streets freely. My only hope is that when mom gets out of prison that she just moves away from us all and lives in her own little twisted world. We all are affected so deeply today and I am not sure there will ever be a day when we will be completely healed. But… this is a start.

If you walk away from this book with just one message, this is what I wish it would be: be passionate and vigilant in everything that you do. No matter what the cause, no matter what job, always be vigilant in your actions. Everyone in this world has a trauma that they live through and trials and tribulations that they face on a daily basis. It is not these actions that make you the person you are, but rather your reaction to your individual issues. If at any time you feel sorry for yourself because you have challenges, no matter what they are; whether it is being a single mom, coming from an abused home or having little money; I implore you to spend one day in basic training. What you will find is a plethora of stories so much worse than your own that you can't help but be humbled. What you will find is a purpose so far greater than your own. You become part of a collective team effort in which the team can only succeed if every individual puts forth effort. You can make a difference in your life today and every day for the rest of your life. You can choose to use your life traumas as a crutch for failure, or you can choose to use them as a catalyst for success. No one cares about your life more than you do, and if you don't care to put forth the effort to make it the best life possible, then why should anyone else? Being a pessimist or an optimistic is so incredibly contagious to those around you. I have found over my life that at the times when I went into a "poor me" attitude, I never achieved happiness. But when I consciously chose to look at life through my rose-colored glasses and think that my positive attitude can change a few things along the way, I have found my success. We can't change the world in a day but each one of us has a ten meter radius that surrounds us where we can make a difference. You can make a difference today if you choose to, the decision is up to you. Today, this is my ten meter radius where I can directly affect my family. It will be my life's mission to be an advocate for success through hard work and determination. I think this makes me a selfish leader because I get so much joy from seeing others whom I am responsible for, achieve their individual successes. It is as if you are achieving that very same success and this is what drives me so passionately today. It might surprise many, but I don't want to change the way I grew up – which I can't change anyway. It made me the person I am today and I am very happy with who I am.

Chapter 2

1970 - 1987

Abuse is an attempt to control the behavior of another person. It is a misuse of power which uses the bonds of intimacy, trust and dependency to make the victim vulnerable. This is exactly what my mother did to us 16 children for *35* years.

My earliest memory is when I was about four years old. I was in the back of our old green Thunderbird with my brother Ted who was five and my younger sister Holly who was one, and we were going over to Grandma Stephens' house for a birthday party. I remember thinking about what kind of cake she made for us. That was a good day – it was a German chocolate cake. Early on in our childhood, things didn't seem that bad and we actually had a lot of good times. I am not quite sure when our world started fading beneath our feet and can't pinpoint the day my mother was no longer a mother but a warden of her own little prison where we were the inmates. In the early years when it was just me and Ted and a couple of the other kids, we had quite the normal childhood, or what I think was a normal childhood. The good days started getting more and more sparse with every child that was born. As the bad things started to happen, we didn't know they were bad. We just thought that was how normal families lived.

The first memories of abuse differ from child to child but for the most part they started when we began cleaning at midnight every night in the family cleaning business. I was about four years old when my parents started taking me and my brother Ted to various establishments; from bars to movie theaters or casket companies; to clean. Our routine became rather predictable. We were locked in our black, hot rooms whenever we weren't at school and when we weren't cleaning. We would go to cleaning every night at midnight and then directly to school at Hoover Elementary. After school we would be forced to march from the garage to the bedrooms where we were locked in until my father came home from work to give us our jelly sandwiches for dinner. That was the routine day in and day out except for weekends when we were in our rooms all day. Our rooms were our dungeon cell and we had no escape. The girls' room was about 10x 13 with two sets of bunk beds and a white dresser with a small black and white television on it. There were no lights in the room as it was forbidden to turn on a light; my mother liked her house dark and gloomy. Our windows were painted black and nailed shut with a shade pulled down over them. Once the door was closed and locked, the only source of light was the television and a small stream of light under the door from the hallway outside our room. That prison cell is where we spent our years and years of solitude. We would sit down and dream about the day we would escape. We would count the days until we turned 18 when we knew we would be free. Unfortunately, I kept a diary and one day my mother found it. Before the day the windows were permanently painted black I drew a picture in this diary. I drew a picture of what the world looked like as I peered out the window in our room. I drew trees and the street and the birds in the sky. I am not sure why I did this, but she found it. She found it when I was about 12, when I had approximately 2038 days left until I turned 18. That diary brought me solitude and escape until she found it. I was summoned to the first floor of the house and subsequently berated with vulgar obscenities from my mother about how cocky I was to think I would ever be allowed to leave. She called me names I cannot put into print or even say to myself, simply because of the emotion I feel when I hear or see those words. Linda, my mother, told me I was going to die in that house and I was beaten for drawing the picture and counting the days. My room was searched on a regular basis for that type of contraband: my contraband of paper and a pencil. I think felons in prison are even allowed to write on a piece of paper, but not in our house. We weren't even allowed to go to the bathroom while we were imprisoned in our rooms. We would pound on the doors to be let out and scream down the air vents that we "really had to go". The response, if any, was "hold it". Well we mastered the hours of the pee pee dance but inevitably our bodies would give out and we would have to urinate and defecate in the bedroom. We would try to hide it by peeing in a pile of clothes or in a bag of garbage so we wouldn't get beaten. The boys were lucky, they managed to pee down the vents and holes in the walls, but the girls couldn't do that, so we did the best we could. The things that happened in those rooms are simply devastating to me today.

The best way to tell the whole tale is to describe some of the stories in somewhat of a sequential order to paint the picture of our home as I remember it. You will see how over the years things got progressively worse. Many of the situations I remember revolve around significant time periods in my life such as a birthday or holiday. What I remember most from all of the birthdays I had while I was young, was dreaming that one day when I was 18 I would go get a birthday cake. This was something we never saw much as our birthdays came and went. The last happy birthday celebration I remember is when I was four years old when we went to Grandma Stephens' house. When we were younger we went to Grandma Stephens' house for holidays, but not without first receiving a threatening briefing on how to act, what to say, and how to respond if asked certain questions. Our entire visit would be scripted by Mom and we were her child actors and pawns. She played on sympathies so

Grandma and Grandpa would give us money for Christmas, but of course it went into Linda's hands. Grandma and Grandpa caught on after a few years and quit giving us money. Much later, after I left home and had my own relationship with them, they told me how much they had wanted to spoil their grandchildren, but knew Linda would take everything. They often cried about it, because as it happened, when they started to question Linda's tactics, we were never taken there again.

Jan 8, 1978 – My 8th Birthday -- The last celebration I can remember is when I was four years old and we went to grandma's house. For the life of me, I can't remember celebrating my birthday ever again after that. Four years later, on my eighth birthday in January of 1978, my mother was mad... very, very mad at me. I can't even remember what for and she was in one of her psychotic moods. She had so much hatred for me and I just didn't and don't know why. Maybe it was because I was the oldest daughter or because she didn't want a girl. Maybe she blamed me for her failure to do something with her life -- she always told me her life was ruined once I was born. I just don't know and I don't think I will ever understand her. Starting with my birthday this year and following with the next two birthdays after that, I was locked outside in the backyard in the middle of a Wisconsin winter, naked with only my underwear on. The back patio had a mini spot where the snow had melted but the rest of the backyard was covered with perhaps a foot of snow with only the tracks of a few stray rabbits visible. I sat my naked self down on the freezing stoop and would get into the fetal position and try and take my feet off the ground. I got so cold so quickly. I hated this. Even my tears froze to my face. How could I have been put out here like this? My ears, fingers and toes would lose feeling next. I would alternate putting my hands on top of each other and brought my elbows close into my body to try to retain some body heat. Now my backside was completely numb, but I was afraid to stand up because now I couldn't feel my feet either. I would wiggle my toes to keep them moving and then my mind would take over. I sat there thinking of Florida and how wonderfully warm it must be. My body wasn't numb from the cold, but it was tingling from the rays of the sun. I loved Florida, how warm it was in my mind. Instead of wallowing in pity for myself I would make myself believe that my tears were beads of sweat. This would go on for hours. My mom really, really hated me and she made no bones about it. I don't even think she realized it was my birthday. I sat outside in the freezing cold wondering what I did as an eight year old girl that would be cause enough to toss me naked in the snow piles for sport by my own mother.

1978 -- Running away to Hoover – By the time I was eight years old I had already had enough of the beatings and the verbal abuse. My mother had told me I would be the child most likely to commit suicide. She would put her nose next to mine and grind her face into mine telling me how ugly and pathetic I was. She called me names I had to look up in a dictionary at school. She screamed in my ears that no one would ever want me and I should just kill myself and get it over with. I wanted to leave and at the time I did not want to save anyone but myself.

Over the years we learned how to escape from our locked cell of a room, sometimes without being detected. Early, early one Saturday morning, I managed to sneak downstairs after they mistakenly left our room door unlocked. I crawled ever so quietly down the stairs carefully avoiding the squeaks in the steps. I went through the living room and got a small suitcase from under a chair and some chocolate bars from my mother's secret stash she kept for herself in the kitchen. I stayed close to the walls and moved at a snail's pace so as not to attract her attention. I can't remember whether other kids were in the house. I told no one of my plan. I packed some clothes and the candy bars and escaped from the house and ran as fast as I could to Hoover Elementary where we attended school just up the street. I hid in one of the doorways facing the nearby apartment complex not really knowing what my next move would be. It was a Saturday morning so the school officials wouldn't know I was there until Monday. I didn't have enough chocolate bars to last until then and I didn't know where to go or what to do. I just knew I had to be out of the dungeon and I didn't care what the cost was. I started eating my chocolate and tried to come up with a master plan in my eight year old mind. I crouched there for about 2 hours when I slowly came to the realization I would have to go back. I knew what would happen when she found out I had tried to run away... but over the years we learned to brace our body in such a way so when we got a beating we could lessen the feeling of the blows. We often compared the marks on our bodies to decide who got it the worst. I usually won that contest. To say that mom didn't like me very much was a distinct understatement. When I decided I would have to return to the dungeon I ate every piece of chocolate I had swiped so at least I could have a full stomach when the beatings began. I gathered my little green suitcase and ran back home. I snuck back in the house the way I had escaped and went back upstairs. She was still sleeping; she didn't know I was gone, oh my God! I wouldn't get a beating and she never knew I had run away. It is a secret I kept from everyone in the family and didn't tell anyone until today.

Jan 8, 1979 – My 9th birthday -- I had another date today, a date with Jack Frost that is. My mom was doing laundry or something and I just remember the piles of dirty clothes being taller than I was at nine years old. I think somebody lost their socks this year and I got yelled at for it and beat across the back in one of her wicked rages. When she looked at you with those eyes -- we called them the bug eyes -- you knew what was coming. She was out of control and she beat you with anything she could reach and hit you anywhere. She didn't even try to keep the bruises out of sight. This time she used a huge metal slotted spoon and beat my hands. I am looking at the scar now and can just see my fingers swelled up with blood and fluid so bad that they were triple their size and I couldn't bend my fingers. Then I was stripped naked, yet again, and sent out into the backyard with the snow drifts. The perimeter of our yard had large trees to shield what happened back there from roving neighbors' eyes. I just remember a lot of snow that year…. a lot of snow. I had become really, really good at wiggling my toes to keep them warm so they wouldn't freeze. Just now I realize that perhaps that is why I do so well in the military -- I had 17 years of boot camp with my mom as the abusive evil drill sergeant from hell. She would close the patio door and curtains and then bring the other kids to see me locked out there. She often used me as an example and told the other kids that if they did not listen to her exactly, this would happen to them too. I can't remember how long I was out there that time. I think for a couple of hours. I just remember that I couldn't feel my limbs when I was allowed back in.

1979 -- Surgeries for drugs – As I look back, this story simply makes me angry that a human-being would do this to another human-being much less a mother to a daughter. My mother had me have two surgeries on my left foot. I think I was about nine during one of them, in fourth grade specifically. It caused a deformity I deal with to this very day in the military and every time I look at my foot, my anger is renewed. I wish I could sue the doctor for this, but the statute of limitations is over. I am sure my mother talked him into it with her master manipulating ways. My mother could talk anyone into anything and make them think it was their own idea. She convinced grown business men to part with tens of thousands of dollars for a great "investment" saying that their money would double in a year. The money never doubled, the money only disappeared.

Well, when I was young I had a bunion on my left foot. My mom took me to the doctor and demanded surgery. She convinced the doctor that I could not live another day without having my foot operated on. I was only allowed to shake my head yes even though I was begging for help in my eyes. Mom would tell the doctor how shy I was and didn't like to talk to strangers as she gave me the look of "if you say anything to contradict me, your ass is mine". Now on the surface, this appears to be a very nice thing - a mother wanting her daughter to have foot surgery for a perceived ailment - doesn't it? I even remember the doctor saying that I should wait about six years to have the surgery because my growth plates were still moving. But damn if she didn't convince him that it couldn't wait another day...there was a reason she wanted me to have the surgery. I came out of the anesthesia and the pain was incredible. They had put three pins in the bones in my foot. They gave me pain medicine and I actually enjoyed my few days in the hospital. God it was nice. I got to sleep and I ate anything I wanted. The nurses brought me ice cream, and it was great, but then it was time to go home. I had a cast on up to my knee and got a prescription for painkillers which my mother immediately filled. She then took all my pills from me and used them for herself because she was addicted to pain medication.

She has been for as long as I have known her. She took so many drugs it took up three shoe boxes. I was prescribed Darvocet and Percocet and she took them all, and the story gets better. I writhed in pain from the swelling and the pins in my foot. I cried all day and all night and could think of nothing else but the throbbing in my limb. I would bite down on anything I could to help relieve the pain and weeks went by before I saw relief. Then she had me go back to the doctor. She forced me to tell the doctor that I needed more pills through various threats of abuse and beatings. She forced me to tell him that Darvocet was the only medication I could take and it was the only thing that would ease my pain. The doctor saw the anguish on my face, noting the pain was genuine. He wrote me my prescription. Mother took my pills once again. I hated that woman for that.

Then to make it worse, so much worse, she did the same thing again a few years later, but this time she had the doctor put a six inch pin straight down the center of my big toe. I left that hospital in tears. I knew what was coming, and I knew I faced a long couple of weeks of gutting out my battle wounds with nothing to ease the pain. How could a mother do this? How could a mother enjoy seeing her eldest daughter scream in pain every night, propping her leg straight up in the air so the blood would drain from her leg. And she sent me back to the doctor again and again for pills. I hate her for that. Then, as if it couldn't get worse, when the cast came off and my mother was beating me for some absurd reason and I was sent running upstairs to my room; one of the nails popped halfway out of my bone and stuck straight up out of the top of my foot. I screamed in terror seeing this and from the pain in my foot. I begged her to go to the hospital, but she wouldn't take me. She merely smirked and said I deserved it. I couldn't put on shoes. I couldn't walk on my foot without sharp shooting pains that still happen to me today. Three days later, she took me to the doctor and he removed the pin and gave me another prescription for the pain. I never saw those pills either, but mom did. How can I call this woman a mother? She is a monster, just a wicked, mean, monster.

In October of 2002, while stationed at Fort Sheridan, IL and pregnant with my son, I saw the doctors at Great Lakes Naval Hospital because I could take the foot pain no longer. For years and years I gutted out the pain and did my road marching, did my running, and did everything I had to do for the military with pain that was indescribable. I was good at working through the pain, it was the way I grew up. In 2002, enough was enough. It felt like I was walking on a knife every moment of every day. The doctor was amazed and couldn't understand how I could ace my physical requirements on the foot that I had. They took out the screws two days later. I now have deep scar tissue on my foot and no movement in my toe and the screws are out, but my toe hasn't grown since I was in fourth grade so the deformity and scars will be with me for a lifetime. About the only good thing I can say is, my life growing up has taught me to bear pain to an unbelievable level.

Jan 8, 1980 – My 10th birthday – Another year, another birthday, another round with the frozen prison on the back patio. This was a rough one and it is something we still talk about to this day. It was my 10th birthday and I was babysitting the kids that day. Mom and dad went out and I was supposed stay home and watch Holly 7, Elizabeth 6, Chip 4, Roger 3, and Ricky 1. Mom was pregnant with Suzy at the time and I can't remember if Ted was home or not. I remember watching television and falling asleep. When mom got home she noticed that the hearth on the fireplace was broken and had a crack down the middle. Not one of us knew how it had gotten there (I think it was the house settling and she first noticed it at this point). Well, as soon as mom walked in the door and saw it she started going ballistic. Holly told mom I had broken it, I got my birthday beating and was locked outside again.

As the years went by I asked Holly over and over why she blamed me on this occasion. My next younger sister often blamed me for things that went wrong in the house. She said, she just didn't want to get beaten. In our house it was survival of the fittest and I cannot be mad. The kids tried to protect themselves from the wrath of her anger, intimidation and abuse. If someone else was getting the beating, then you weren't. Ted was also a favorite to blame. We were the oldest.

80's – The teen years -- These years were tough. The situation inside the home was bad and my days at school became more and more difficult. Not only was I a teenager going through normal teenager stuff, but I was going through it under my mother's obscene reality and control. I was ridiculed mercilessly at middle school for the way I dressed and wore my hair. My mother was obsessed with me being miserable and forced me to wear my long hair in two pigtails on the side of my head all the way through middle and high school. She insisted I wear clothes which belonged to her (she was several sizes larger than me) or forced me to wear formal dresses. Everyone else wore cords or even jeans. She never allowed me to wear a pair of pants. I was forced to wear a skirt every single day. Every single morning when we got home from cleaning she would tell me what skirt and what shirt to wear. I never got to choose. I was her puppet. God forbid I put on someone's makeup. When I reached my high school years, she often showed up unannounced in the middle of the day just to check up on me and she bribed Holly to get her to report me if I had broken one of her rules once out of the house.

80's – Ted's beating in the basement tied up to the pole – from Jennifer's perspective – This is a poignant memory in my mind. This is the quintessential example of how mom intimidated, manipulated and controlled us through tactics that even enemy combatants sometimes do not face. My mother should be facing prison time for this act alone against her own child.

Being the oldest children, Ted and I often took the brunt of the abuse from Mom. One day when Ted was about 15, he did something inexplicably wrong; he probably asked to go to the bathroom or something. Well mom, in a fit of rage, stripped him down to his underwear and tied him to the red pole in the basement and started whipping him with the humidifier cord. Her psychological warfare technique was to call all of us kids down to watch. She would say things like "this is what happens when you don't follow the rules" or "this is what happens when you don't listen to me". I can't imagine for a minute what was going on in her head. Time after time after time, she forced us to watch as she abused the other kids. She was nothing short of a monster and we wept for Ted that day. We all shed tears for each other during such events. God help us if we tried to stop it, then we would have been strung up on that very same pole. From what I could tell, she enjoyed doing this. She took so much pleasure and utter pride and joy in bringing us pain, how could I call this woman mother?

Jan 8, 1983 – My 13th birthday -- I remember this day well. My mother was a master manipulator and this story sticks out in my mind. You could actually meet my mother on the street and think she was an angel and that all 16 of us kids made up anything we ever said about her. On this day mom took a couple of us to the Natatorium in Milwaukee where you can have lunch while watching a dolphin show. Now, on the surface this does seem like a wonderful thing to do for a daughter on her 13th birthday and that is exactly what my mother will tell you, but here is what happened. On this day mom took my father's parents with us to this event for my birthday. My Grandpa and Grandma Stephens were very trusting and as I stated, mom was a master manipulator. Grandma and Grandpa wanted so much for things to change, much like we kids do today. Every time she would be selling a story they hoped it would be true, hoped that she was changing her ways and making life better for our family. But instead she duped my grandparents out of hundreds of thousands of dollars and this was the way she did it. First, she took them along to witness what appeared to be a huge act of kindness; where she donated what she claimed to be thousands of dollars worth of Avon supplies to a local Goodwill. (As a sidebar to this, my mom was an Avon representative, but it was part of an elaborate scheme somewhat like check kiting. She would "buy" 50 crates of Avon supplies and then turn around and return them for money. Other times she told Avon she hadn't received the supplies so she would receive double shipments. She then used said Avon supplies to give to Goodwill as tax write-offs.) Mom took my grandparents along so that they could see how wonderfully generous she was. Next, she invited them to lunch with us at the Natatorium to talk to them about this "big plan" she had where she would make thousands upon thousands of dollars and all she needed was some seed money. Now my grandparents are witnessing a woman who donates to the poor, takes the teenage daughter out for her birthday to a great restaurant and is now merely asking for them to support her in a huge financial endeavor. My mother made up these grandiose details about what she was asking them to fund and how could you not believe her? My grandparents were unsuspecting, untrained and were promised a huge return within the year. I think my grandparents lost $50,000 that time.

Jan 8, 1985 – My 15th Birthday -- Yet another event that takes place on a birthday. As I stated before, for years and years I kept telling the kids that one of my wishes when I turned 18 was to get a cake for my birthday. Well little did I know that this would be the day it would happen.

My mom was angry at me again, for what I do not know. I think I was referred to as the devil child that day. Plus, she had heard about my big master dream of having a cake for my birthday so she grabbed me by the hair and dragged me into the downstairs bathroom. She made the kids stand at the door while she pushed my head over the toilet and smashed a chocolate cake in my face and hair and said "You want a fucking cake, here is your fucking cake." and told the other kids to quit asking for things, otherwise this would happen to them too. The part my mother does not know about to this day, is that we joke about this event a lot. After she kicked me in the legs and punched me in the back, I was smiling. I was smiling at the other kids as I licked the chocolate cake off of my face and said "at least I got some cake". I almost enjoyed that moment. I pretended to be upset, but secretly I was happy I got chocolate cake on my birthday. I think we as kids try and cover the bad memories with things like this. I really think that is why I always look for a silver lining in the storm clouds. There is always something good in something bad. I and my sisters had many laughs in our black-windowed room over this incident. We masked many moments of pain with moments of laughter.

80's – Crusts -- Not every memory of our house is bad. In fact, we learned to make the best out of every situation and this is such a story. In the late 70's and early 80's, on the rare occasion when we were locked outside the house instead of inside, Ted wanted to play baseball and none of the girls wanted to participate, just because we had no strength. Ted was the oldest followed by three girls. As you can imagine, we had very different ideas about what we considered to be a fun activity. He tried brut older brother coercion, but it never worked on us. There was one thing; however, that Ted found did work. When we got our stack of jelly sandwiches slid out the patio door, much like a prisoner receives food through the bars in his cell, Ted would take his sandwich and give us his crusts. There were eight crusts on each sandwich and each girl got two crusts to play a certain amount of innings with enthusiasm. Ted would hit the ball and we all played the field until we felt we had played two crusts worth. Ted would even work on the I.O.U. system and sometimes we wrote it down, "Ted owes Jennifer, Holly and Elizabeth 4 crusts each." It is amazing what will motivate you. Now that I think about it, I think later he was able to get the younger boys, Chip and Roger to play ball without paying them but never the girls. That is a good memory.

Early 80's - Iron cooking in the bedrooms – This is actually quite a funny story and something I and a couple of my sisters were able to pull off for quite awhile. Even after we were found out, we lived high on the memory of how long we were able to go undetected. Over the years of being locked in the bedroom, we figured out a way to unlock the hook and then relock it so my mother never knew we left the room. I was watching our black and white TV one day (For whatever reason, mom gave each room a tiny black and white TV. I think it was to keep us occupied so we wouldn't bother her with menial things like having to go to the bathroom – I think she saw it as a built in babysitter.) when in an episode of "One Day at a Time" the teenage girls warmed up a piece of pizza on a clothes iron. My eyes glistened as my thoughts raced. This was something I was going to have to try. So, we snuck up an iron, bread, butter, and cheese and started our first experiment, a grilled cheese sandwich. It was the best sandwich we had had in a long, long time and we were so excited. We propped the iron upside down with the ironing plate facing up, kind of like a college hotplate. We cooked our concoctions using the food we were able to swipe on our rare escapes from our rooms and savored the fruits of our labor. We snuck up chicken bullion and made some chicken broth and we even brought up spices to make it interesting. My dad would come up the stairs and smell something cooking so we would throw a pile of clothes over it and scramble to our beds. He would ask us if we had anything in there but we put on our innocent looks and said the smell was coming through the vents. I think we made it about six months before we were found out. One day, we were caught red-handed. Dad had tiptoed upstairs and all of a sudden the door swung open, but I think he was rather shocked to see what we were doing. He told mom and well, we saw her terror. But even after the beatings, hair pulling, and an inability to breathe from the kicks in our stomachs; we smiled at our accomplishments and imagined what we would cook if we got the opportunity again. That memory kept us going for years.

70's thru 80's – stealing lunches – One of the poignant memories I have, when someone in the school system could have made a difference, was when I was in elementary school. All through grade school I resorted to stealing lunches for food. I would sneak them into the girl's bathroom and eat the evidence. One day I got caught and was sent to the principle's office. I actually didn't care what the principle was going to do to me; I was completely terrorized by what my mother's reaction would be. There was only one way I was going to survive and that was to lie. When the principle asked why I had done it, I told him it was because I was hungry and he told me he was going to call my mother. So I started sobbing in his office and begged him not to call. I think I told him she was pregnant and in fragile health and that news like this would cause a miscarriage. Somehow he believed me and didn't call her. I promised not to steal another lunch, tragically cutting off my supply line of food. In hindsight, I wish that principle would have called social services and reported the incident. I don't know if it would have solved any of our problems, but it certainly was an indicator of what was happening at home.

70's through 80's -- Eating out of the Garbage – This is definitely a story I am not proud of, but a story that has to be told nonetheless in order to understand how we became survivalists in our family. We adapted to whatever situation was thrown at us regardless of the severity. Dad worked all day and it would have taken an act of God for mom to get off her sacred couch in the family room and make a sandwich for us kids. We never were allowed to touch the food. God forbid we would put an extra piece of cheese on the sandwich, she maintained control of everything, all the time. During summer vacation from school, we often did not eat from the time dad left for work to the time he got home. In the winter, at least we had school (when we were allowed to go) to break up the days. In the early years before we became permanently locked upstairs, we were often locked out in the backyard. We took our naps and took care of kids in that backyard or we snuck out to the local gas station and stole treats. When we got beaten for sneaking off somewhere and were too scared to leave the yard, we would go to the trash can right outside the gate. Of course first we would have to climb the fence and jump over because there was a padlock on the other side preventing us from leaving any other way. Once we mastered the jump, we would scavenge through the garbage, remembering that mom had had one of her gourmet meals of breaded pork chops and mashed potatoes. She rarely cooked the meals herself, she always had dad serve her. On the very rare occasion she did take a place at the stove, it was for herself and only herself. On occasion we would come across her scraps and the pork chop bones in the garbage, but we had to wipe off the maggots before we could eat it. I don't think we fully understood the repercussions of what we had to do to make our stomachs feel full. Some of us even ate grass, but that grew old quickly. We ate anything we could get our hands on including old hard ketchup sandwiches found under a bed. We would just wipe away the bugs and eat our food. One time when we were cleaning, we found an old hamburger under a movie theater seat and thought we had hit the lottery. That was a great hamburger that day.

Strangely, I remember my mom always calling me fat and in my mind that is truly how I remember myself. However, as I look at the photographs today, I get physically ill at how emancipated we all were from lack of food and proper nutrition. She was very good at mind control and still is to this day. Some of us kids have real food and self-esteem issues and my hope is that these issues aren't passed on to our children, but remain only our misery and daily fight.

Late 70's or early 80's – Prescription fraud – I will never forget this situation for as long as I live and as I think back to it, I cannot understand how a mother could put her child through this. My mother started altering prescriptions when I was very young, perhaps five or six years old. Mom would get her prescription of choice for either herself or for Dad. For Dad she always had a ready prescription for Ritalin from one of the kids. She repeatedly had us lie to the doctor in order to get a prescription so she could keep him awake all night to be up with her. (Dad was the victim in this situation because he would work all day and then try to get a three or four hours of sleep before he had to get up in the middle of the night to clean. However, my mother would take those precious few hours between 9pm and 1am away from dad to keep her company since she was such a night owl. She would make him take her for car rides, go gambling at the local bingo parlor or go out to restaurants. During the day when he was at work, she would sleep to recharge for the next evening.) Sometimes she would get prescriptions for pain killers. She would get Darvocet and Percocet. Those two drugs were her favorites and for as long as I can remember she was addicted. She always had a pharmacy on the table near her makeshift bedroom in the family room. I think she fabricated many things in her mind and enjoyed the "high" she received from the painkillers. After a few years, she was so addicted that without them, she became quite ill. In fact my mother concocted a story where I was allergic to codeine (when my mother put me through surgeries, codeine would be a painkilling drug of choice for a person my age and my mother knew it would not be strong enough for her) so she could have stronger drugs prescribed for me. When she would get the prescriptions, the doctor would put a 1 on the refill line but before mom turned it in, she would buy all sorts of pens and markers and try to match up the ink to the prescription. She sometimes had 20 different pens to sample before finding the right one. Then she would change the 1 to a 4 with the stroke of a pen and turn it in to be filled to get her fix. Then of course, no one but she got the pills regardless of the ailment. She took them every single day. Sometimes, I think to knock her out. Well in 1980 or there about, the police caught on when the pharmacy reported irregularities. They called her in for questioning but before we left for the station, she acted all nice and sweet to me. She acted the mother I longed to have every day. She told me she was going to take me somewhere nice to eat if I would do her a favor. She scripted a story I was to tell the police about how I forged the prescriptions for no apparent reason whatsoever. She then followed up that if I didn't do it, there would be consequences to be paid and I feared what would happen. Now don't think the police bought that story for a minute. They questioned me alone, but all I pictured was a nice dinner and no beating. The police said, "We know you didn't do it, but you have to tell us who did." I couldn't. Sometimes I look back and think maybe I could have made a difference back then. Maybe I could have changed history, but it will remain a mystery. Without evidence that she forged the prescriptions and with all the blame on me, they had to let her go. One of the prescriptions she altered was that of her OB/GYN who delivered most, if not all, of her kids. Mom took painkillers during every phase of her life, even during the many years that she spent pregnant with my brothers and sisters, but she didn't want to be embarrassed for getting caught for this so she had me go to his office. She scripted another conversation where I was to admit to the doctor my wrong doing and say that I would never, ever do it again. I look back at that and wonder how he could have believed that story too. So many times things could have been caught, but this would just remain another story for me to tell. I never did get that dinner she promised, all I got was a trip back up to the room.

70's and 80's – Second mother -- Taking care of the babies was my role in my mother's eyes. Not once while growing up do I recall her not pregnant nor can I remember her changing a single diaper or hugging a child even once. In fact, mom used pregnancy and pregnancy fabrications to abuse the existing children and as a way to gain attention from extended family and even bystanders on the street. I firmly believe that one of the reasons she had so many children was for the attention factor, but I have no proof. Mom would say every pregnancy that she was pregnant with twins. Inevitably, somewhere within the pregnancy she would fake an "episode" where she had a miscarriage. She used this to gain sympathy and attention from my aunts and uncles and even to get out of paying household bills on time. Mom would then use the supposed "miscarriages" against us children. She would blame us and name our evilness as the reason for "losing the baby" and say that the death of our unborn brothers and sisters would hang over our heads for life. She used guilt to bring us into submission. Because she hated me most, I was personally blamed for at least five miscarriages of babies that never existed. We knew with every pregnancy with more certainty that we would be getting one of these stories. In fact, when mom announced she was pregnant, we wouldn't believe it until we actually saw her come home with a baby. She was so heavy you really couldn't tell if she was pregnant or not. When she did come home with a baby, they would be dumped in the girls' room if they cried. Sometimes I would have three at one time; one on one hip, a second on the other and a third in between. I really didn't mind taking care of those kids. I think I raised about eight of them myself. So many times I remember the babies crying from being hungry or wet. I would put clothes on them as diapers if mom refused to give me any spares and I remember laying on the bottom bunk with the babies on my belly and just rubbing their backs and soothing them. I remember pacing back and forth in between the bunk beds for hours at a time. I learned so many of my parenting techniques from those moments. I learned that diversion is sometimes the best medicine for hunger because the mind can be so powerful. I tried to make the babies laugh or I would just rub their backs for hours and hours as they lay next to me. They got to eat at the same time we did, which was few and far between and it makes me cry when I allow myself to think of those kids. My heart aches to this day when I think of those rumbling stomachs.

I do remember Dad doing a lot of diaper changes. He always made a big production out of the poopy diapers and made us laugh so hard. I do some of the same things to this very day with my son. Dad would really play into having a stinky diaper and yell out, "Toilet paper!!!!! Someone get the toilet paper!!!!!!" Then he would put the roll of toilet paper under his nose and proceed to change the diaper making all sorts of noises of embellishment to the task at hand. It was so funny. It was moments like that which endeared our father to us so much. He was so much more paternal than mom was ever maternal. Dad was good with the kids when he wasn't tired and the babies hung onto him when he gave them his time.

Taking care of the kids like I did made me feel more like a mom than a sister. Every single day it would be me and my sister Holly's job to get the kids ready for school. We would get home from cleaning that morning and get all the kids dressed the best we could with what we had. It was always great to get ready for school because we knew we would get a few hours in the world on our own without her wicked ways. We would change the babies and give them some love and affection before they were left to fend for themselves. When we got home from school later in the day they would be our first priority because we knew that they didn't get much during the day, a diaper change if they were lucky. That would only happen if dad stopped home for lunch or if mom had one of the older kids skip school in order to take care of them. Holly and I were usually the ones tagged to skip school to be the mother of the house. It was not unusual to spend a total of only 80 days or so in school during the year. Mom would call us in sick, sometimes a week at a time with rare diseases we never had just to stay home and be the mother. One night while we were playing this roll, I remember walking into the babies' room to check on the kids after cleaning and was just horrified at what I saw. There were no lights in the room because mom wouldn't allow it, so I only had the glimmer of light from the hall. All I saw was blood. There was a head sticking out of the sheet with the hair all chopped up with bald spots and what I thought was red blood all over her head. It was my sister Lisa. I started screaming and pulled her out of bed and into the hall to see what happened. She must have been two or so and when I brought her in the hall she cried because I screamed. In a flurry, I started to look for the source of the blood when I realized it wasn't blood at all. One of the kids had shaved her head and put red lipstick all over her head. I was so scared for her, it was just awful but at least it turned out okay. To this day I don't know which child did it, nor the reasons behind it. I am sure it was just innocent experimentation but it kicked my maternal feelings into high gear. Like when we would be all locked in our separate rooms and the babies would be crying in one room and I would be in the other. It was some of the most heartbreaking moments I can remember. The babies were so helpless, locked in their room, no one taking care of them and they would just scream. I would lie at the bottom of my door where there was about a ½ inch crack between the door and the carpet. I would sing at the top of my lungs so the babies could hear me down the hall: everything from "Twinkle Twinkle Little Star" to endless rounds of "Row Row Your Boat". I would do anything to soothe those kids. The more I think about those moments, the more I despise my mother for treating her children like trash. To this day, I just don't know why she kept having children if she hated us so much and wouldn't take care of us. Mom often joked about me being the second mother for the kids. I am not sure how she got "second" mother when I felt like I was their only one and I never understood why she found it to be funny. She never cared for those babies like I did. It was so easy for me to take care of them. It really wasn't an effort and I would do the same thing today given the same situation. I thank God for my conscience and I thank God that when I look at my two children today I can't help but say "I love you" every day. I thank God that my brothers and sisters knew they could go to their older brother or older sister to look out for them. I thank God that I left when I did and set the example for the other kids to follow. I think my emotional ties to so many of my brothers and sisters are why I fight so hard for them now and with such vigor.

70's thru 80's – Mom and Dad's marriage relationship – Mom used dad at her whim and often treated dad like a dog. This was awful to witness and incredibly emasculating for Dad. I am not sure you can say that my mom and dad had a traditional relationship per se. I would rather try to explain it by describing the different ways mom controlled dad on a daily basis, every minute of the day, in every facet of his life.

From the stories they told over the years, I really do think it started out as a typical young love relationship when they began dating. They talk about those early days before they were married with fondness and tenderness – it was almost enviable. I really do believe that when mom started having kids that is when their relationship began to change. My oldest brother Ted told me that his earliest memory is dad crying on the front stoop of the apartment complex where we lived because mom had kicked him out. I think control is the factor that is at the root of evil in my mother's actions. She always has to have the control. In fact, other than her appearance in court on July 27, 2005 when she was sent to federal prison, never once in my life had I ever actually witnessed with my own eyes her not having, or attempting to have, control of a situation. Another odd fact is that I have never known my mother and father to share a room together, much less a bed. I guess I hadn't considered it odd until I really sat down and thought about it. From my earliest memory, mom had her room in the house but that did not last for long because early on in my life she had taken up residence in the living room and family room for sleeping. Her bedroom became a storage area for the things she wanted to be kept locked up away from the children or out of sight – we were never allowed in that room. I never in my life remember my dad sleeping anywhere in the house except in the hall outside our rooms. He was banished to the floor by mom every night of his life. I can't understand why he allowed that to happen. I think it is sad that I cannot remember my father sleeping in a bed my entire life. Mom would talk to dad every night about the work he did during the day at his day job. She would have him reconstruct his conversations word for word. She would then script how he should respond to those conversations the following day. She controlled his success and failures every day. This too I cannot explain how dad allowed to happen, I can only speculate that it started out with a husband telling his wife about his day and a wife giving some suggestions about how to handle something. Then, something twisted occurred where mom needed to relive every moment of dad's day and work out how he should handle the events of the week. Dad worked two jobs, the family cleaning business at night and his day job of course, and by the time he finished working, he had already worked an 18 hour day easily. Then mom would feed him the Ritalin to keep him awake during her night-owl drives and conversations and if he dozed off, she would ridicule him mercilessly and would feed him more pills. She cared not one ounce for his welfare. She went ballistic when he fell asleep and she lost control of him. By the time dad finally got to sleep, only an hour or two would go by before he would have to do it all over again. Dad tried to sneak in a catnap anytime he could. I am still heart-broken at the memories of my dad sleeping in the car in a parking lot or while waiting for a light to turn green. In order to stay awake while driving he would stick his head out the window and yell "yyeeeowwww" at the top of his lungs on the freeway just to get his blood pumping to stay awake. To this day, the license plate on my vehicle says YYEEOW in tribute to his resolve and I get to tell that story every time someone asks me what it means.

Sometimes mom would get so angry with dad that she would go after him physically. She would beat him in front of us and throw things at him. Dad never hit her back, he just took it all. She abused him over and over and when she was done she would kick him out of the house. She would throw all of his things on the driveway or sometimes she would burn them. Dad would be forced to go into the backyard and yell through the window with the air conditioner in the family room. He would stand outside and beg mom to let him in while mom had us sit on the floor and she would sit on the couch or the pull out bed and just laugh at him. She would say "no, go away" just to hear him beg some more. I cannot figure out why she got so much joy out of this. I suppose it was because she wanted everyone to know she had control of everything in our lives – even our father. He would be at that window begging to come in and for forgiveness, but in my opinion, he had nothing to be forgiven for. She did this for sport. Sometimes mom would use us to pass her messages along. She would have us tell dad how awful he was and if we didn't repeat word for word what she wanted us to say, we paid the price ourselves. Sometimes the words were said through tears when we saw our father treated in this demeaning manner and our hearts ached with pain on his behalf. As a young teenager, I wanted to save him from his own wife. She so enjoyed his pain and never once, never once showed remorse for her actions.

Sometimes mom would even fake an injury to herself or even go so far as to inflict an injury on herself and say that dad did it. She would get a bruise by hitting something and then blame dad for it. She tried to turn us against him so many times. I truly, truly think she was jealous of how many of us felt about dad and that we did not harbor those same feelings for her. I think she felt better about herself when she tried to make dad look worse. Her only problem was that it backfired. We only became more endeared to our father in his times of despair. The thing that will leave me wondering for life is how and why did he put up with it all of those years? Why didn't he leave her or at least stand up to her? Dad would be a psychologist's dream case (not that mom wouldn't be too in her own right) because somehow this grown man allowed this life to manifest itself right in front of his 16 children. I can't even begin to describe the sex life, or rather my mother's demands to be serviced and her use of sex as a weapon. Sex was an event that was orchestrated and controlled by her, and not discreetly. Out of respect to my father, I won't describe this part and will leave it at that.

Even in the act of medicating him, she treated him like a dog, her personal play thing. She would make him kneel down in front of her with his hands behind his back, his head tilted back with eyes closed and had him stick out his tongue. She would drop pills in the back of his throat so he would be awake with her all night. Sometimes dad took the pills and hid them under his tongue or spit them out, but mom caught on to this tactic. Poor dad was somewhat of a victim himself. I think he suffered a form of battered spouse syndrome, but we never got him to see that. While driving to cleaning, we asked him why in the world he took what she was dishing out. He kept saying he was going to stand up to her – but that day never came. We hoped every day it would, but it never did. Mom wouldn't even let dad take a shower in the house. He was forced to shower at cleaning. He even had what we kids affectionately called a "nerd bag". This bag was where he had to keep all of his personal hygiene items. When dad finally did speak up for himself once in awhile, we kids would be so happy someone was standing up to her. We cheered him on from our listening posts. Then, when mom started to beat him on the back and head, our hearts sank as we saw our mother tearing down our father right in front of us.

The worst, absolute worst, was when we saw dad cry. It didn't happen often, but I can probably count 5-10 times that he broke down. You can't know how that feels until it happens. My loyalty to him only grew. Mom constantly accused dad of having an affair. For years and years she would harp on him and dad had to continually defend himself. Amazingly, I found something in the public records in Waukesha County from 1987, exactly one month after the kids were taken away. According to court records dad filed for maintenance (divorce action) from mom. I don't know what happened, but I can imagine. He probably tried to leave her and she lured him back in. I don't think I will ever know the truth about that one and I can only speculate.

I had the opportunity to talk with dad one time in the last 18 years while mom was in jail in 2004. In that conversation I was frank with him and told him I loved and missed him and that I both condemn and commend him for his loyalty to Linda, his wife. I said if nothing else, there is unconditional loyalty to her, but it came at the price of his 16 children. I, as a mother, could never choose my spouse over my children, and I will never begin to understand his loyalty to her. I have however come to terms with the fact that he will never leave her until one of them dies. I am not sure my father has love for my mother, but rather, I think he feels he is committed to her. I can't remember a time when dad said he loved her; I will always wonder about that.

80's – Numbness, Disassociation, Repression and my father – After years and years of enduring the things mom put me and my brothers and sisters through, we became nearly immune to the physical torture. In fact, we almost were happy when we got the beatings, because we knew it would be over soon enough -- we preferred it over every other form of punishment. In contrast, Mom's verbal and emotional abuse antics caused scars so much deeper. And we were so distraught after the psychological beatings that they seemed to have much longer-lasting effects than merely getting beaten in the back. We came to know that mom's sole purpose in her eyes was to tear us down to nothing. We expected it; sometimes we even believed it. It took years and years to fully realize it wasn't true and even today I am haunted by her words from years ago.

The physical abuse or the threat of physical abuse which incited the fear in us occurred over years and years. It had dramatically negative effects on self-esteem for so many of us. As we grew up witnessing my mother physically abusing our father, us and our siblings, fear became an underlying feeling within the home. Because of this some of us developed a problem with dissociation as a means to cope with our own overwhelming feelings. When I describe what happened at the hands of my mother, it seems like it happened to someone else and is just a dream to me. I simply dissociate and separate one part of my inner-self from the other parts. An example which many have heard about and perhaps can relate to is post-traumatic-stress disorder (PTSD), most commonly seen in war veterans. Many suddenly begin to have flashbacks, to waken in the night shaking, sweating, or screaming, or avoid certain people or places and begin to withdraw from their loved ones. In our case, PTSD was the result of the war zone in our own home. The ability to dissociate has become a part of my personality and an art I have inadvertently mastered. To this day it serves me well in the military. No matter what training we do in the military, it is nothing to me. No one can yell at me hard enough or tear me down far enough. I disassociate and simply drive on with what is expected. Disassociation can be used adaptively, to survive trauma, or maladaptively, to avoid feelings, both of which I am guilty of today. I am a survivor of mom's wrath of anger and intimidation, but I am also guilty of avoiding any type of relationship where I am not in control. I am not sure I will ever recover from that feeling. I am not sure I will find someone who can share my life, given my past.

Previously dissociated memories sometimes come back to me when my brothers and sisters start talking about the past. I can't remember the scenarios until the stories are being told and then it is clear as day what happened and I see it replaying over and over in my head. I repressed so much. One example recently came to light. I didn't remember this event until my oldest brother Ted reminded me. He witnessed the following situation. I had done something to anger my father. I can't even tell you how old I was but he grabbed me by the hair and started beating my head into the refrigerator. I blocked that memory for decades and even now when I describe it, I am disassociated with the memory - like it happened to someone else. The worst part is, I love my father and I truly think I repressed every bad memory I had of him because he showed me so many moments of kindness. Dad would sometimes try and make the most horrible moments bearable; he would try and lighten the blows of physical abuse. He would soften the emotional abuse and say mom didn't know what she was doing, or he would say, "You know your mother, just let it go in one ear and out the other." Dad would throw money on the floor, simply to let us find it so we would have a stash. He would sneak food to us or take us to a gas station for a treat. Dad was always trying to make things easier for us, at least that is the way I remember him. Over the years I always said that if mom died, I would instantly go back to dad to help him raise the rest of the kids. That day certainly never came nor will come. The point is, I truly can't remember many horrible memories of dad and maybe I repress it because I don't want to remember those moments from the man I loved. Repression is another one of the mind's many ways of protecting itself. This repression has given me the walls I need to survive and succeed today.

Mid 80's -- Holly cutting her hair – As I said earlier, not all of my memories are bad. Along with my father's diaper changing antics, we also laughed when Holly's hair was mysteriously cut in the middle of the night. We were forced to wear pigtails in our hair until we were taken out of the home in 1987 (yes, I was a 17 year old forced to wear pigtails to high school every single day). One day when it was time for school Holly came sauntering downstairs from her room. One pigtail was normal while the other one was mysteriously cut off about two inches below the top. Holly said she saw me cut it off in the middle of the night (which of course wasn't true) so instead of mom going ballistic at Holly for not being able to wear pigtails, she went ballistic at me. Knowing full well how much my mother hated me, Holly made sure my mother would take her vengeance out on me instead of her. I had no clue what had happened but mom would not listen through her screaming and Holly got to wear her hair short for awhile. We laugh today at how easy it was to get mom to believe I did everything. I don't believe the kids enjoyed seeing the repercussions, but remember, we lived in a time of survival and if you weren't the one getting hit, then you were the one surviving.

1985-today – Meg Without this person and her mother, I am not sure I would be here today to tell this story. Margaret Possell was my best friend in High School and she knew just about everything that happened. She was always there and was a friend beyond compare. I could never go to her house, I could never come to her parties, but when we stepped foot in the high school every day, she was the face I looked for to get me through to the next day. From my daily trials and tribulations in my first three years of High School to the last year where my world changed forever, she was there every day. There was no pity, there were no tears, there was simply a smile and a shoulder to cry on. She has never looked down on me nor has she ever asked me for details. She simply listened to my stories and offered me help like it was no trouble at all, like it was something that just had to be done. I don't remember to this day how I met her or how we became such good friends, but she is someone I can call and say something to and she is never shocked. We just laugh and know there are more chapters in our book to be written. I thank God for her – if she wasn't in my life, I am not sure I would have made it through. Thank you Meg, I am not sure if I really ever thanked you. I will never be able to repay you, and the best way I can keep trying to is by being there for someone else like you were there for me.

Here is a message from Meg:

< MEG'S ASIDE: At this point many may be questioning my friendship to Jenny and asking themselves how a good friend could refrain from reporting the abuse, but the truth is that Jenny was very good at keeping most things to herself. I thought it was rough that she had to work all night at the family business, but I figured if that was what paid the food bills, then that was her family's decision (little did I know that she rarely was fed). I tried to help her get through the classes she slept through and fudge the homework she never did at home. Of course many of the stories of her mother's obsessions sounded odd and we wondered why Jenny wasn't like the rest of us, but for the most part everything seemed plausible for a family of 12 or 13 (at the time). It seemed normal for a mother to be a control freak when she had so many children to care for. It didn't seem strange that Jenny often missed school to help out at home. We went to a private catholic school and it wasn't unusual for kids to have very strict parents.

Naturally when abusive events became evident alarm bells rang, but they were singular events spread out over two years. Once, I threatened Jenny and said I was going to turn her dad in when she showed up at school with a strange bite on her arm and her leg slashed open from a coat hanger, but she pleaded with me. She said her family was the only thing she had in life and that no foster home would take 12 children – she was right. When I didn't back down, she said she would say I was lying and as a 13 year old without any evidence I felt helpless. I did what I could for Jenny. I did what she would let me.>

Having read this, I have to say that I am deeply indebted to Meg. I feel like I owe her an apology for the way I acted, but then I remember the fear in my head at the time. There was so much fear of retribution that I had to drive away those that I cared about most and those that cared about me. Meg provided me an escape during those years and I just appreciated it for what it was; an escape for a day, not a lifetime.

1985 -- Running away to church – A second time I tried a real escape. When I was about 15 and mom kicked me out of the house yet again, I took it to heart and left. This time, I packed nothing and I didn't stop at the Hoover door wells. I ran to 92nd and Greenfield Ave which is about 5 miles from my house. I just remember walking and walking and walking until I had to stop for the night. I saw a church on the corner and knew that was my place of solace for the night. However, it was somewhere around 10:00 p.m. and the doors weren't open. So, I sat on the steps, laid my head on the door and slept as best I could with my arms inside my t-shirt for as much warmth as I could muster. I was scared sleeping under the stars and just kept thinking about what my next move would be. At that moment in time, I wasn't going to go back home, but it was freezing outside and I was cold. Fortunately across the street there was a 24 hour Laundromat which has since been replaced by a Subway sandwich shop. I went into the Laundromat grateful from the warmth of the dryers. Surprisingly, there are lots of people who do their laundry in the middle of the night and one gentleman approached me. Now picture a 15 year old girl wondering aimlessly through the night being approached by "some gentleman". I was scared. Looking back, that was extremely dangerous and I am glad I didn't realize it while it was happening. He asked me what I was doing out and I told him a just a little bit of the story. We talked while his laundry was being done and when he left all he did was leave a quarter on the counter for me to call home. Believe it or not, he wasn't the first or the last person to tell me that someday I will forgive my mother, but not that night nor any night have I been able to find it in my heart to do that. I also, quite frankly, get upset when people so flippantly tell me to forgive and forget. How can they say that? It is impossible to make people understand why that is an improbability. I can't imagine I will ever forgive and I simply can't forget what that woman did to me, my brothers and sisters and my father. The one hope I cling to is that someday when she meets her maker she will come to realize the magnitude of her actions. I think if we should meet in the afterlife, maybe then there will be forgiveness - but not today.

After this encounter I left the warmth of the Laundromat and sat back on the church steps. As the morning sun began to rise and I was exhausted from lack of sleep, I began analyzed my situation and begrudgingly began to walk back home. As I walked with my head hanging low, I knew what would befall me when I got there so I tried to prepare myself. I got home, knocked on the door and the garage door opened. In I went where I received my gratuitous beating in the head and back. Linda screamed profanities at me for leaving the yard and yelled that when I get kicked out of the house I am not to leave the yard. I was sent to the dungeon of my room and the spiral continued.

1985 -- Mom started having us work and taking the money – As Ted and I became older teenagers she had us get jobs and then she would take our paychecks from us "for rent and subsistence" she said. Todd got a job working for my uncle at his custard stand in Hales Corners, WI. He would work there many days during the week and mom would collect his check every two weeks to supplement her spending habits (on herself, not on necessities for the children). I worked there on occasion too, but I found a job babysitting for a local auto shop owner who was a single dad and a friend of one of my teachers at Pius high school. Most of the other kids ended up working at the McDonalds down the street. We often joked that if McDonalds was short an entire shift they could just call the Stephens family. We kids liked working because we got food. Turning over the checks to mom was just a given. Sometimes she would tell us lies like she started a college savings trust for us, but little did we know, there was never a savings account. We were her little slaves but we had freedom when we went to work. It was my babysitting job that I was walking to that day when my world came crashing down before me in September 1987.

1986 – 1987 - Going to Marquette University for mom – My mother claims quite often that she was a nursing student at Marquette University in Milwaukee and in fact she states it in the police reports to the New Berlin Detective in 1987. Sometimes she even fabricated stories about being a traveling nurse, I think for attention. What she won't tell you is that she never went to the classes, instead, she signed up for the classes and sent me in her place. My attendance records from Pius XI High School show that I was absent well over half the year. I was rather academically inclined and I think my mother saw an opportunity to take advantage of that. Starting in my sophomore year of High School, she called me in sick to school and instead dropped me off at Marquette University by the nursing school (ironically next to the Army ROTC building) with a notebook and a tape recorder. My instructions were to tape the classes, sign her into the class and take copious notes. If the instructor asked where she was, I was given an elaborate story of pregnancy complications, medical issues or family matters which demanded her attention. Mom would listen to the tapes at home and read the notes and only show up the day of the exam. I learned a lot in those two years. I took pharmaceutical classes, nursing classes, diet and nutrition, and philosophy in Lalumiere Hall. I actually learned more than I bargained for. Wouldn't it have been nice if I had gotten credit for those classes I attended? I could have been a nurse by age 20. Sometimes there would be a couple of hours between classes where I would just sit in the courtyard watching the college students go by. It was my time of freedom where she didn't have her hold on me. It was almost like a second life where I was just a normal person. I am not sure why no one ever asked why a 15 year old was in college, but they never did, so I kept going without any resistance. I learned about the heart, the mind and nursing in general and I even got quite bold in some of the classes. The instructor would be soliciting answers to questions and when no one would answer, I would stand up with a very meek raised hand and answer the questions about cardiac procedures. I got the very strange and curious looks and smiles of recognition and astonishment that someone so young knew the answer, so I studied more. I think that is the reason why I place such an importance on academics to this very day. I can't stop going to school and continue to be in academics just for fun and security. The fact that the military offers so many opportunities to get an education, well it is perfect to keep building my background. I even want a PhD. As I went through my MBA program, I had a smile on my face for the entire two years because I couldn't believe how easy it was. Maybe I should thank my mother for sending me to college for her; however, then again I am incredibly thankful that she never graduated. Can you imagine her working on a patient when she never went to the classes? This behavior was considered normal by her. I often wonder what the school would do to prevent this from happening in the future. To this day, I still don't know how she was able to never go to class, then show up on test day and pass. The only explanation I can come up with is that she had a very good note-taker.

1987 – This undoubtedly became the worst year of my life up until this point – It started with Chris, a person my mother forced me to date when I was a junior in high school. Mom would use her threats and intimidation to get me to do everything she wanted me to do with this guy. She scripted every conversation I was supposed to have and every time I was supposed to "run into him" at school and how to react to it. She had me say certain things to "spark" his attention; things I never should have said. I suppose I could have just been mean to him and it would have never happened, but I didn't know any better at the time and I was scared. Mom lived up to her threats which is why the fear factor was so high. Chris embodies such an embarrassing life moment, but it is very critical in understanding why I harbor so much resentment towards Linda for her actions. Mom was a master manipulator.

She was the master in doing whatever she could to get whatever she wanted. How this relationship ever started, I cannot remember for the life of me but it is something I wish never happened. Chris went to high school with my sister and I and his dad was rather affluent in Brookfield. I am convinced mom was trying to get me or my sister involved with this guy to get to his father's money, but it is nothing I can prove. She forced me to have a physical relationship and at 17 when I came home crying that some kid put his tongue in my mouth she told me to shut up and do it again. She forced me to doing things with this guy I can never get back. She gave a 19 year old boy cases of beer, Heineken to be specific, to take advantage of her 17 year old daughter, and that is how I remember my mother to this day. In the passing days my mother would make me sleep at the foot of the couch and she would talk about it to people on the telephone in graphic detail and made me listen in silence. She was a disgusting mother who didn't care about her daughters' innocence. Quite the contrary, in fact, when I ran away and after all of the court cases ended in 1988 and the kids were returned, she forced Holly to go out with him too! I do not know what happened in that relationship and I will never ask although I have my suspicions. I do not fault the guy in question, he was just a teenage guy who thought he had some easy action. Little did he know he was merely a pawn in my mother's world.

September 14, 1987 -- This is a day I will never forget; it was the day I looked into my mother's eyes and saw my own mortality. It was the day I wanted to give up trying and just pass away to the next world. This day is engrained in so many of the kids' minds. Each child that witnessed it can tell you a story of psychological warfare, utter pain, mental anguish, and overall defeat. This day was worse than anything I have faced in 14 years in the military. This day was worse than anything I could imagine, it was the day my mother tried to kill me and the day that I saw the devil in her eyes. So much of the last 17 years had built up to this moment and this day was merely the straw that broke the camel's back.

This day started like any other day in our house, but it ended being a day that changed our lives forever. After school that day I was walking to my babysitting job which was a couple of miles away. One of the sneaky things I did as a teenager was to switch my clothes and hair when I got to school. Mom always made me wear those skirts and two pigtails in my hair (I think she was reliving her high school years through us), but I snuck a pair of pants to school and a brush. When I got there in the morning I would go to the bathroom and switch out of my skirt and comb out my hair. Ted knew what I was doing but he never said much; he knew the deal. Well, I took my skirt along with me, but when I was walking to the house where I baby-sat I was still wearing my pants. Unbeknownst to me, my mother was following me in the car. One of the controlling tactics she had was to arbitrarily show up somewhere to spy on us. She would follow us around to see what we might be doing behind her back. She often told us we were being followed, even when we weren't, to keep us afraid of her even outside the boundaries of the house. Whenever we got caught doing something she did not like, we paid the price through beatings and degrading screaming tirades. Well this particular day, I got caught. She saw me wearing pants and I had my hair down rather than in pigtails which was one of her number one rules. She shoved me in the car and made me take off my pants and threw them out the window. To this day I do not remember how Mr. Maloney found out I wasn't going to be baby-sitting for him anymore. I think I was in too much shock to remember that. In the car she started to beat me in the head and saying things to her 17 year old daughter I can't write down on a piece of paper. All I could do was cry to myself, but I thought it would be over soon, until we stopped at the hair cutters. She said that since I cared so much about my hair and I wouldn't wear the pigtails that she would have it cut off. She had my father who was driving the car, take me in and say "cut it short" and then they left me there to get it cut. I cried in the chair the whole time and told the lady that my mom was forcing this. She cried too and said she would try not to cut too much. My dad came back to pick me up, looked at my hair still reaching clear down to my lower back and said "your mother is going to be mad". I tensed because I knew what was coming. I got home and no sooner did I walk in the door that the bug eyes my mother is so famous for came out and she went straight for me. She was so mad that she ran over to me and started pounding on my head and my back. I screamed in pain and disbelief and this went on for a while. Then she went even more crazy, if that is possible. She made dad get my sisters Holly and Elizabeth down from the room to watch what was about to happen. She wanted them to witness what would happen to them if they dared to disobey or go against what she ordered. Mom dragged me to the bathroom by my hair, held my face up to the mirror and screamed profanities at me. Next, she took me by the neck with her forearm and strung me up on the wall so that my feet dangled. She had freakishly strong grips you couldn't get out of and she made the girls watch as she terrorized me. I screamed and the girls screamed for her to stop but she wouldn't. She pushed on my neck and put her face up to mine and yelled "Do you want me to kill you? Do you want me to kill you now?" and the only words that would come out of my mouth were "yes, yes, yes just kill me now and get it over with". She dropped me and yelled at the girls to watch what would happen to them if they ever disobeyed. She took a knife and started chopping off my hair to the scalp - just chopped and chopped in her fit of rage and beat me to my knees. I drained of life in that very moment.

When she was done she sent us all to our black prison cells of our rooms and the girls cried for me that night. I slumped down on the bottom bunk, curled into the fetal position and prayed to God that I wouldn't wake up.

September 15, 1987 – the day I finally left home – After falling asleep in my locked black room in an endless pit of sorrow and despair, the time came to go to cleaning. I was to continue on like nothing had happened. My dad called into my room to get up and get into the car to go to work. I hadn't seen my hair myself yet because I had no access to mirrors after the assault. I felt my head, not sure if what happened was a dream or if it really happened. I cried, I just kept crying. She took the one thing from me that I adored, my long beautiful hair. I looked like a boy and to this day I can't bear to have short hair because of the memories associated with it. I sat in the car with my head on the window feeling lifeless and I had no ounce of hope. I was done, I was finished, I wanted out of my life. I continued on with cleaning, just working through my silent tears unable to look at my father who allowed this to happen to me. How could he let this happen to his daughter? After cleaning my mother made me wear a wedding-type dress to high school with my tattered hair, most assuredly used to distract from my head. She slapped me a few more times when she saw the tears on my face and cut my hair some more, to even it out she said. I just stood there, emotionless, feeling dead to the world.   I was dropped off in front of school. Tears formed in my eyes as I noticed people staring at me walking through the halls. I walked to my homeroom and then walked right past it. I didn't know where I was going, but I wasn't going to class like this. I hid in the sixth floor bathroom. I stared at my hair. I crawled under the sink into the fetal position and just started to cry. People came in and asked me what was wrong, but all I could say to them was, "go get Meg – I only want Meg". Someone understood; someone got her. To this day I don't know what I told her. I blocked so much of what happened. Someone gave me a bandana to put on my head and she took me to the chapel in the school basement. She brought in Father Reiney, a new priest at school (more on him later) and I told them everything. I was hungry and pulled out my lunch and ate the spaghetti sandwich that was packed for me. Meg and I shared a laugh about that one. She stayed with me all day – she is my hero, she saved me.

After I told the Father everything he brought in a Nun, Sister Ruth I believe, and they discussed my options. It was decided that I should first go to Pathfinders, a shelter for runaways on the eastside of Milwaukee. They wanted me to stay there, but I refused. They said I could legally be gone 24 hours from home before someone could go out looking for me. I had to find shelter for that night, somewhere where I would be safe. Before I even got to say a word Meg said she would take me home with her that night. I was so scared at what was about to unfold before the both of us. We ended up getting on the bus to get to her house in Wauwatosa and suddenly she and I were embarking on our first adventure. She laughed at me on the bus because as we left Pius and traveled through the town I remarked, "oh my gosh, the street signs are blue". I never knew that the street name signs were any color other than green. We never left our little area in New Berlin. That night Meg and her mom welcomed me with open arms but the peace did not last too long. My mother found out that I was at Meg's house and she camped out in her front yard and started yelling at the top of her lungs. The police were called and I sat upstairs crying and in complete terror that she would take me back home. Meg and her mom did everything they possibly could to console me and they said that they knew someone down the street and that they were going to get me there. Poor Jane, Meg's sister, was left to endure mom's psychotic ranting and raving on the front lawn. They just got a small taste of the life I was living everyday. I was snuck out the back door and we ran down the street like we were in hiding from the enemy. We made it to the other house where I made a very important phone call. I hadn't talked to my dad's family in probably a decade when I called Uncle Butch and Aunt Judi in tears. I told them who I was and that I ran away from home and asked if I could stay there for the night. I can't remember what else I talked about but I ended up at their house where mom would never suspect my whereabouts. From what I was told my mother stayed on Meg's front yard for most of the night. I can't remember reintroducing myself to my relatives but looking back, I am so grateful they opened that door for me. They have been suedo parents to me for the last 18 years and I am awed by their selfless acts of kindness that night. As the next day started there would be no school for me. I got up and had breakfast like a normal person. I sat at the table and served myself a meal, something I had not done in 17 years. Aunt Judi and Uncle Butch listened as I poured out my life story at the breakfast table and they told me some of the things that I never knew about my extended family. Later that day, Father Reiney came to get me. They had worked through the night looking for an option that would save me. This was the only option I had and ironically enough, mom's escapades from the night before at Meg's house were enough to get a restraining order. Fr. Reiney told me they would take me back to Pathfinders and they would protect me for two weeks. I started to cry. I just started to cry and couldn't stop. I think I said yes I would go and off we went. Fr. Reiney drove me there and I told them about everything that happened in my home and then they gave me another blow. They said they could only let me stay at Pathfinders if my parents gave permission. My world sank again, how could I escape? She would never give permission! I would be found out. I would be in the most trouble I have ever been in and who knows what would happen. I said as much. I told them every word mom would say to make me out to be the liar and the evil one. Word for word I described how the conversation would play out. I even shocked myself at the level of detail I provided. They called her on speaker phone, and nearly word for word it played out exactly as I predicted. Somehow, someway those administrators convinced her to let me stay. Thinking back, perhaps she had no choice. If she had nothing to hide, why shouldn't I be allowed to stay. I was still in my dress - she demanded it back. She demanded the clothes off my back. I borrowed some of theirs' from a donation bin and they handed the dress over the next day. I don't remember where I slept that night. I don't remember much of anything except that it was the one of the first times in 13 years I hadn't had to get up to go to cleaning.

Father Reiney at Pius XI High School – I have blocked out so much of my high school years; so many things that my mind has tried to protect me from over the years. A sad part about that reality is that I have little memory of the man who risked everything to save a family. Father

Escape from the Dungeon

Rieney was an integral part in our lives changing and for me to escape the dungeon. I am saddened that my memories are not clearer. Father Rieney was new to Pius XI; so new in fact, that I think it was only his first or second semester in the school when we crossed paths.

Have you ever started a new job and jumped into a project, not fully realizing how mammoth the project was until all was said and done? You just did it one element at a time without seeing the vision of the project, just your vision as the person accomplishing it. Then later you look back on the project and only then begin to realize the size of the task you were able to complete. The premise behind this question is that sometimes, it is easier to tackle the tough tasks and issues when you don't really have a full understanding of the magnitude of the complete task at hand. I think Father Rieney looks back at what happened and sometimes wonders how he got sucked in and then was able to make such a drastic difference. He accomplished something no other had been able to accomplish before he came into my life in 1987. I hope to find him again one day and tell him just how grateful I am. After all, as describe earlier, my mother had built a reputation for philanthropic donations to the school for whatever reason. All of the administrators knew of her donations and contributions but I don't think Father Rieney did. He was too new. He didn't know of her desired status within the community and therefore was not intimated nor influenced when I told him my story. Maybe that is what it took, someone unbiased, someone who would believe me for the words I was saying and not try and defend her somehow because on the surface, she appeared to be the tireless mother devoting her life to her children. What Father Rieney unknowingly did was to go straight for the heart of the hornet's nest without fear of retribution or retaliation and without intimidation. When I sat in his office on September 15, 1987 he listened. He listened to me through the tears and he heard the terror in my voice. He showed me genuine concern both as a human being and a priest I was confessing my life to. I think it was when I was seeking counsel from him on that day that he became my second savior after Meg. This man knew nothing of me before I was brought to him and immediately potentially sacrificed himself to save me. I shutter when I think what would have happened if he didn't listen. It was because of him and his unconditional belief in me that I became so attached to the church, its beliefs, its morals and ethics and find comfort in the pews. If he hadn't listened, I wouldn't be surprised if I had followed through with my suicidal thoughts and met an untimely death. I don't remember much about Father Reiney's role after those first initial days. Everything is such a blur. I am grateful to him for taking a stand against my mother. I hope that all said and done, he would choose to do the same thing over again. Hind sight is 20/20 but I have to say, I don't think he could have handled it any better than he did.

(As a note, I am also happy there was a place like Pathfinder in existence and applaud the talent of the social workers there. They are doing their daily part in changing society one youth at a time.)

September 16-22, 1987 – Pathfinders – Over the next week I told everyone everything: about the abuse, about the cleaning, about mom. Today everything is such a blur. I told them I would tell them everything if they would leave well enough alone. I just wanted to escape. I couldn't save the others yet, I just wanted to escape. They interviewed Ted too and I talked to him for the first time in months. He was shocked at what had happened, but he was supportive, thank God. He was shocked because all the time we grew up in the house, we all planned to just run away when we turned 18. Never in his life did he think I, or anyone else for that matter, would have the guts enough to turn mom in for abuse. I think he was shocked that I had the strength and courage to actually defy her in such a huge and grandiose manner and at the level of defiance and "no fear" attitude I mustered up (not that I wasn't scared out of my mind). Ted too was in a state of shock, but he shared his stories like I did. In fact, Ted was the one to bring up the fact that mom had a gun with live ammunition laying next to her makeshift bed in the family room at all times.

I lived at Pathfinder home for runaways those first two weeks and could see mom watching me from the window. She would drive back and forth in front of the house and all I could see were those "bug eyes". I just knew she was going to get me good. I would crawl under windows so she couldn't see me walk past and I hid low in the cars as we were driven to school. I was so scared to go to school. I was so scared mom and dad would show up and snatch me home.

Then, the day came just before the kids were taken away. On the evening of September 21, 1987 I was told of the "no-knock" search warrant that would take all 12 remaining children away. I screamed deafening screams and started beating my wrists against the fireplace at the home for runaways. I wanted to hurt myself so bad because I knew this was all my fault. I was out of control. The workers just stared, because they knew they couldn't stop me. They called the police who looked at my arms all swollen, bruised and bloody and restrained me. They said if I didn't stop hurting myself they would take me away. Whatever they said, I stopped. I sat by the phone because the police said they would call the moment the kids were out. I think I got the call about 4 o'clock in the morning. All the kids were taken to the police department. All of them were in shock. I was told they were given food,

Jennifer M. Stephens

drinks and toys and that they were all very happy to eat. I can't remember the exact time I saw the kids again. I just can't remember when I saw them next after all of that. Everything is so blocked from my memory I can't even remember if I saw them in the next couple of days.

September 22, 1987 - No-knock search warrant – After hearing everything that went on in the house from Ted and me, Waukesha County obtained the above mentioned no-knock search warrant at 2:00 in the morning to take the children into protective custody. Here is what they found on that day in the words of the investigating officer in a report filed with Waukesha County Courthouse on October 2, 1987:

1. The downstairs portion of the home was extremely cluttered with boxes, clothing, books, knick-knacks and garbage. The bathroom was dirty and the bathtub had scouring powder in it. The kitchen was cluttered with dirty dishes, some of which still had food on them. (Getting the dishes done in the house was not an everyday occurrence; we used paper plates, but when dishes were used, they were stacked up until dad was given time to do them. The bath tub had scouring powder in it because sometimes that was what we used as soap to get clean. There wasn't soap in the house to wash ourselves so we used whatever was available and we figured if it cleaned the sinks well, it would clean us as well too.)

2. The upstairs portion of the home consists of four bedrooms and one bathroom:

*a.   In room #1 (**girl's room**) two sets of bunk beds were found, the light switch was taped over with duct tape and a door lock, the type operated with a key, was found on the door. This* *lock was situated so that it could only be locked from the inside. No one was sleeping in this room.*

      b.   *In room #2* (mom's room – dad never slept here) *apparently the parents' room, boxes and clothing were observed. No one was sleeping in this room.*

      c.   *In room #3 the boys' room, a lock was observed on the door, again with the keyhole to the outside. A piece of duct tape was attached to the door and doorjamb. Four boys were sleeping in this room. There was no operable light in the room. Two sets of bunk beds were in the room and the windows were nailed shut. The curtains were drawn and could not be opened. The beds had sheets but were observed to be dirty. A garbage bag was found in this room that was filled with dirty diapers and other garbage.* (In the boys' room everyone was in shock as the police came in to take them away. Some of them just were in disbelief they told me later. Everything in their room was from day to day living, just garbage bags full of garbage and diapers.)

      d. In room #4 (baby's room) police observed two young girls sleeping on one single mattress and a third sitting on the floor. Two of the girls were wearing only diapers. The girls on the mattress were wearing only diapers. The mattress was covered with a dirty sheet. The door to the bedroom was locked and could be opened only from the outside. There was no operable light in the room. Two television sets were found in the room one of which was playing and providing the only light from the room. The odor of urine and excrement which emanated form the room was bad enough to force one police officer to leave the room and go downstairs to avoid being sick. Feces had been smeared on the walls of the room. (In this room were the small babies, ages 8 months to three years old or so. They were forced to fend for themselves and had no adult supervision. The only supervision they had was when the older kids would look out for them in their respective rooms)

2.   *Police found a handgun and bullets in a small ice chest in the family room.   Police reports indicate the gun was readily accessible.* (This was the gun mom kept in the house along with twelve bullets at her bedside – a few of us contemplated her motives and Holly even said she thought that there would be grave repercussions if something bad went down. We try not to think of what she was planning to do with it and am grateful the police went in when they did. Twelve kids' lives may have been saved that night and I simply thank God for that).

3.   *Police found Elizabeth asleep on the floor of the dining room, Jeffery in a crib in the laundry room where a television was playing and Holly awake in the family room caring for a younger sister (*Remember, it is 2:00 in the morning. Dad was in California for a business trip and mom was asleep on the couch. Jeffery was only 8 months old sleeping in the laundry room and Holly was 15 at this time with one of my sisters in her arms*).*

It has been additionally reported to the Department by Ted Stephens, an adult sibling of the Stephens children, and by Jennifer Stephens that all of the children are routinely locked in their bedrooms and that the windows in these room are nailed shut or covered, even in hot weather. The children are allowed out of their rooms two times per day to use the bathroom and are given their meals in the bathroom or in their bedrooms. Additionally, the children are not allowed to have lights in their rooms and lights and/or light bulbs are confiscated if found by the parents.

Jennifer also reports that on September 14, 1987 both of her parents physically restrained her, pushed her face into a wall and cut her hair. Her mother also struck her on the jaw, near her ear, and asked Jennifer if she wanted to her kill her. Chip also observed this and reported it to petitioner.

Chip reports that he has observed his father bite Jennifer on the hand on two occasions, once during the cleaning outings. He also reports seeing his father hit Jennifer in the face while she was driving the car.

Jennifer also reports that she has been forced to drive the family car, even though she has no driver's license. She states that this occurred when she was asked to take part in the family cleaning business.(As I remember it, I think this started at the time I was about 14 years old. I was never taught to drive, I was simply told to drive and had to learn along the way what I was supposed to do. As you can imagine, that was pretty scary but I picked up on it quickly and I soon became a driver for the family even though I was not licensed.)

Sometime after this incident and prior to September 22, Jennifer ran from home. She was located at Pathfinders for Runaways in Milwaukee. She had not been reported missing by her parents.

Ted reports that in December, 1986, Jennifer, Holly, Elizabeth, and he were forced to go outside without shoes or a coat for approximately 1 and ½ hours until one of them confessed to stealing cookies discovered missing by the mother.(This situation is rather famous among us children. Mom was simply fanatical about her food. She was very possessive and we were never allowed to touch anything of hers. She counted everything from her candy to her cookies. Well, one day she found one of her Pepperidge Farm cookies missing, not a bag of cookies, one single cookie. She brought all the kids down from their locked rooms and lined us all up and interrogated us all on who took her precious cookie. None of us admitted to it, although often one of we three older kids would take the fall for something like this, but mom was going ballistic at this point. She grabbed the 8 month old baby and pulled out a thick leather strap and threatened to beat him senseless until one of us admitted to taking the cookie. Mom loved this form of torture, bringing us all into submission through terrorizing the little kids in front of us. When none of us admitted to taking her cookie she ripped off the baby's diaper and began beating him until someone admitted to taking the cookie. Holly risked her own life to save the baby by taking the blows while Ted or I admitted to taking the cookie that we never did. Then we were all locked outside in the cold for our wrongdoing that day.)

It has also been reported that the older children, including Jennifer, are forced by their parents to work between the hours of 1 a.m. and 6 a.m. for the family cleaning business. During these hours, the younger children are left at home alone, locked in their rooms.

In another report filed on September 24, 1987 by a Waukesha County Social Worker:

As of September 24, 1987, eight of the oldest Stephens children and the adult brother have been interviewed individually by the Department of Human Services and the Police Department. Each child interviewed to date has reported similar instances of being locked in their bedrooms for extended periods of time (sometimes without supervision of anyone over the age of 5) and at other times with the adolescent children present in the home but locked in their rooms.

Each child reiterated being disciplined by use of a belt, bath brush and coat hanger for looking out windows, asking to go to the toilet and breaking family rules. At times a single child has been physically disciplined in front of the other children for purposes of gaining information.

The children have also reported defecating and urinating in their rooms as a result of not being allowed to use the bathroom facilities. The children report not receiving regular meals during periods of confinement.

Oct 28, 1987 – First set of criminal charges – This is it. The first court battle which we still face today, 18 years later.

Below is a reading of the criminal complaint filed against Linda on October 28, 1987:

1. Count

Investigator Philip Kiedrowski of the City of New Berlin Police Department, being first duly sworn on oath, upon information and belief, says that: between October 29, 1981 and December 24, 1984 at 12340 W. Burdick Court in the city of New Berlin, Wisconsin, the defendants did:

Count #1 – *being concerned with the commission of the crime in that they did intentionally aid and abet the commission of said crime, contrary to Wisconsin Statutes, subject a child to wit: Ted C. Stephens, to cruel maltreatment, contrary to Wisconsin Statutes.*

And further advising the court that the above alleged offense is defined as a Class E felony and upon conviction of the above alleged offense the above name defendant is subject to a monetary fine of not more than $10,000 or imprisonment of not more than 2 years or both.

Count #2 – *same for Jennifer*

Count #3 – *same for Holly*

Count #4 – *same for Elizabeth*

Count #5 – *same for Chip*

Count #6 – *same for Roger*

Count #7 – *same for Ricky*

Count #8 – *same for Suzy*

Count #9 – *same for Michael*

Count #10 – *same for Andie*

Count #11 – *same for Lisa*

Count #12 – *same for Mary*

Count #13 – *same for Jeffrey*

And prays that the defendant be dealt with according to the law; that the basis for complainant's charge of such offense is: complainant's personal knowledge and investigation as well as his review of the investigative reports of Officer John Fischer, Sergeant William Miller, Officer Mark Hurst, Corporal Daniel Noordyk, and Officer Michael Jeannotte of the City of New Berlin police Department, and Waukesha County Department of Human Services employees Cecil Roman and Marilyn Krause, all believed in this instance to be truthful and reliable. Officer Fischer's report indicated that on September 21, 1987, he obtained a search warrant for the private residence occupied by the Stephens family in New Berlin, Wisconsin. Officer Fischer's report indicates that the purpose of that search warrant was to obtain custody of the eleven Stephens children amends and identified in Counts #3 through #13, includes of this complaint. Said report indicates that at the time, Officer Fischer was acting upon information supplied by Marilyn Kraus and Cecil Roman of the Waukesha County Department of Human Services that on September 21, 1987,

2. Jennifer's statement:

Ms. Kraus and Ms. Roman had occasion to speak with female juvenile Jennifer M. Stephens, believed in this instance to be truthful and reliable, who had just run away from her parent's residence at the above location. Jennifer further identified her parents as the defendants, Thomas and Linda Stephens. Jennifer reported that prior to running away, she lived at the aforementioned residence with her parents and eleven younger brothers and sisters, and that for as long as she can remember, she and her brothers and sisters have been locked in their rooms immediately upon returning home from school. Jennifer also indicated that the boys' windows themselves are nailed shut. Jennifer indicated that routinely the children and herself were allowed out of their rooms only twice a day to use the bathroom and that they also took their meals in the bathroom of the residence. Jennifer also described a situation whereby she and her older brother and her next younger brother, Chip, would be required to work nights in the family cleaning business commencing at 1:00 am and working until it was time to go to school. Jennifer advised that during the time, the other younger children of the family were left at home, locked in their rooms and unsupervised. Based on the following information, Officer Fischer spoke with Ted Stephens who is currently enrolled in a Waukesha College and living outside the home (Ted was the first to turn 18 and escape the dungeon. Since he was the oldest and mom's pride and joy, he was sent to college and he got to leave the home. Ted moved into an apartment in Milwaukee and gave us all hope of escape when we turned 18). *Ted, an ordinary citizen believed in this instance to be truthful and reliable, described that for as long as he can remember, his parents have locked him in a room with the windows locked. Ted indicated that in the summer months he would lie on the floor next to the door trying to get air because of the heat. Ted also indicated that they were not permitted to have any lights in their rooms and that if a light was on, it was immediately confiscated. Ted also confirmed that they were not permitted to go to the bathroom unless they were let out of the room by his parents. Ted further indicated that they were only allowed to go to the bathroom two times a day, if they were lucky. Ted related that they were given their meals at the same time they were in the bathroom. Ted further informed Officer Fischer that on one occasion in June, 1987 when money was missing out of his mother's purse his mother lined up himself, Jennifer, Holly , and Elizabeth and then laid his baby brother, Jeffery, who was then five months old on her lap and proceeded to spank Jeffery with a belt until one of the older children confessed to stealing the money. Ted related that on September 17, 1987 he went to the house to pick up some supplies for his dorm room and later discovered that both his mother and father were absent from the home because they were seeing a social worker. Ted indicated that he returned later and saw that his sister, Lisa, had a large purple welt on her back that was approximately 9-12" in length and 2-3" wide. Ted indicated that he learned that his father and struck Lisa because she looked out her bedroom window. Ted indicated that this type of discipline has occurred a number of times in his home, especially involving himself and his sister, Jennifer. Ted further advised Officer Fischer that his mother keeps a gun in the house and that on previous occasion when he asked his mother about the gun, she indicated she would use it to shoot herself. Ted indicated that his mother has made numerous comments and gestures in the past about killing herself. Ted further advised Officer Fischer that the gun is kept in the family room of the residence which his mother uses as a bedroom as she sleeps on the couch.*

3. *Search Execution:*

Escape from the Dungeon

Officer Fischer's report indicated that based on that information, it was decided that the New Berlin Police Department SWAT team would be used to execute the aforementioned search warrant obtained shortly before 12:00 a.m. on September 21, 1987. Officer Hurst's report indicates that as a member of the New Berlin Police Department SWAT team, he was involved in executing the search warrant at approximately 2:03a.m. on September 22, 1987. Upon officers approaching the home and knocking on the door a subsequently identified as the defendant, Linda Stephens answered from inside and was advised that the officers were present to discuss the subject of her runaway daughter, Jennifer. Linda Stephens was then observed to open the garage door at which time the officer were able to gain entry. Officer Jeannotte's report indicates that while inside the residence, he located a handgun further described as a Colt Detective Special inside a cooler next to a couch in the family room of the residence. Also in the cooler were found thirteen rounds of ammunition. Officer Jeannotte indicated that he believe the gun was readily accessible to any child in the residence. Officer Hurst's report indicates that it was his assignment to check on the safety of the children in the upstairs residence. Upon going upstairs, Officer Hurst checked two bedrooms on the north side of the home. Upon opening a door on the east side of the hall, Officer Hurst found bedroom containing four boys in a bunk bed, those four boys being subsequently identified as Chip, Roger, Ricky, and Michael Stephens. Officer Hurst noted that the bedroom door was not locked but that it had a apiece of gray duct tape going from the door to the doorjamb. Officer Hurst then went to the door on the opposite side of the hallway and detected a strong odor. Officer Hurst indicated that upon opening that door, he was forced back by the nauseating stench of human excrement, and he was then forced to remove himself to the first floor of the residence to avoid becoming ill. Corporal Noordyk's report indicates that he accompanied Officer Hurst in searching the upstairs of the residence and upon the second door being opened he found three very young female children in the room, two asleep on a dirty single bed and another sitting of the floor. Those girls were subsequently identified as Suzy, Lisa, and Mary Stephens.

Corporal Noordyk further noted that the door leading into the room was locked form the outside and that the girls could not have exited the room if they had wanted to. Corporal Noordyck then went on to check the room containing the four boys and found it to be generally dirty. Corporal Noordyk observed that there were four bunk beds in the room, all with dirty sheets, and that the windows were nailed shut. Corporal Noordyck further noted that there was a garbage bag between the bunk beds which contained dirty diapers, old food packages, and assorted other trash which emanated a foul odor. Your complainant, who was also involved in the execution of the search warrant, remained on the first floor of the residence and located Holly and Andie Stephens awake in the family room watching television. Your complainant also located Elizabeth Stephens asleep on the floor in the dining area off the kitchen. Your complainant further observed Jeffery Stephens awake in a crib in a closed laundry room off the dining area and that there was a small television playing in this room at the time. Your complainant further observed the entire first floor of the residence to be extremely cluttered in that there were piles of clothing throughout the kitchen and numerous dirty dishes in the sink and on the counters. Your complainant then assisted other officers in removing all of the minor children in Counts 3-13 above from the residence to be turned over to foster homes.

4. Children's Statements:

Your complainant states that he has further had occasion to review the signed written statement of Jennifer M. Stephens, believed in this instance to be truthful and reliable, who related that prior to the running away from home in Mid-September, 1987 she and her brothers and sisters had been physically abused by her parents on numerous occasions. Jennifer specially indicated that her parents would use the "little babies" as "truth getting machines". Jennifer indicated that on more than one occasion, her mother Linda Stephens would lay a baby either Jeffery or Lisa, across her lap and spank them with a belt until one of the older children admitted to doing something wrong. Jennifer also indicated that the incident which prompted her to run away involved her getting her hair cut off and when she did not get it cut short enough, her mother threw her up against the bathroom wall and forcibly cut her hair. Jennifer indicated that her mother tried to choke her during this time with her arm and asked her if she should kill her. Jennifer further indicated that her brothers and sisters were constantly locked in their rooms and were only allowed out to go to school and to use the bathroom. Jennifer indicated that on occasion both of her parents would go to Las Vegas leaving herself and her brother Ted to do all of the cleaning and to take care of the other children. (It was common place for mom to leave the older kids at the age of 14 years old in charge of the younger kids for weeks at a time. Sometimes mom wouldn't even tell us she was leaving until she was gone. She would leave long notes of instructions on everyone's duties and the number one rule which was that no child was allowed to go to school while they were gone so there would be no chance of it leaking out that mom was out of town and had left her 10 kids alone to fend for themselves.) *Jennifer further related that lights were not allowed in their rooms, nor were they permitted to do homework in their rooms. Jennifer indicated that it was her opinion that if there was an emergency such as a fire, there would be no way to get out of the rooms because the locks on the doors were on the outside. Jennifer also indicated that they were not permitted to go outside as they please, nor was she permitted to join any clubs as school, wear makeup or have any friends. Jennifer advised that when she wore makeup her parents would call her a "whore", a "streetwalker" and other derogatory names. Jennifer indicated that for as long as she can remember, her mother has taken pills, and that on one occasion she had to go to the Hales Corners Police Department and lie about altering some prescriptions to protect her mother when, in fact her mother had altered the prescriptions. Jennifer indicated that she was told by her mother to go to a doctor and ask for Darvocet when she didn't need it. Jennifer also related that she was required to work in the family cleaning business, often getting up at 1:00am and not returning home until 7:00am in time to go to school. Jennifer also indicated that her parents would not allow them to go to church. Jennifer further advised that her parents would require her to stay home from school when she was not ill to either take care of the other children or to go to Marquette University to sit in on classes and take notes for her mother who has previously been enrolled as s nursing student there.*

Your complainant has further had occasion to speak with female juvenile Holly Stephens believed in this instance to be truthful and reliable, who described for your complainant a typical school day which began with Holly getting up at about 1:00am to go to cleaning jobs with her father Thomas Stephens, Elizabeth, Jennifer, and Chip. Holly indicated that she was willing to help with the cleaning because she was told it was necessary to help pay for her college education. Holly indicated that they would clean all night long and arrive back home at about 6:30 am at which time she would help get the smaller children dressed for school and then assist in feeding the children. Holly indicated that her father would usually make a breakfast consisting of a sandwich and possibly some milk or water which would then be served in the upstairs bathroom. Holly further confirmed that all the children were continuously locked in their bedrooms including Ted, until he left home last summer. Holly indicated that until September 21, 1987, the bedroom doors were locked form the outside. Holly indicated that this was changed the morning of September 21, 1987 before her father went to California (for something to do with business) *because her parents believed that some social workers would be coming to the home because Jennifer had run away. Holly further related that with respect to bathroom privileges, she and her brothers and sisters would have to knock on their locked doors and hope that someone would come and let them out to go to the bathroom. Holly indicated that if no one came, they would have to "hold it". Holly further indicated that at on times the smaller children would have accidents and would be forced to go in their rooms in bags or in the closets. Holly indicated that sometimes her mother tells her not to go to school for no apparent reason and then has her take care of the younger children. With respect to discipline in the home, Holly confirmed that her father does hit them with belts or brushes and that this is done to elicit confessions from the older children.*

Your complainant has further reviewed the written report of Dr. John Iverson, a clinical psychologist, who has had occasion to interview and evaluate Holly Stephens. Dr. Iverson related that Holly indicated to him that she sometimes goes to be hungry as she primarily received ketchup, butter, or jelly sandwiches to eat at home. Holly further advised Dr. Iverson that she has never had a friend over to her house, with one exception, that being when she was in 8th grade and the friend stayed for about five minutes. Holly further advised that she is not permitted to go to friend's home and this is "mom's rule" which she initially thought was normal but has since decided it is not. Holly further informed Dr. Iverson that the main reason for discipline in her home is the stealing of money or food. Holly indicated that her mother usually disciplines, but if she does not want to deal with something, she says, "Tom, take care of it. Just hit until someone confesses." Holly also advised Dr. Iverson that she is not permitted to wear makeup, barrettes, or hairspray, and that she wore her hair in a ponytail until recently when her mother took her to a beauty parlor and got her hair cut short. Holly also related that she feels her mother treats Ted and Jennifer cruelly but that she herself is treated less severely because she baby-sits and is honest. (In this situation you cannot in any way, fashion or form place blame Holly for trying to survive. In our house it was the quintessential survival of the fittest. Holly simply did what she had to do to survive and stay out of the wrath of anger, intimidation and abuse inflicted by mom. I wish I could have mastered evasion like she had).

Your complainant further had occasion to speak with female juvenile Elizabeth Stephens who advised that to the best of her recollection, her normal school day begins at about 3:30am when she gets up and goes cleaning with her father and other family members. Elizabeth indicated that her parents told her that this would help her go to college. Elizabeth indicated that when they finished cleaning and arrive home at 6:30am she would help get the younger children ready for school and help prepare their breakfast. Elizabeth indicated that they all had to be quiet because their mother was sleeping at this time. Elizabeth described a typical breakfast as consisting of sandwiches, crackers, cereal, milk, pickles or leftovers and also confirmed that this food would be served in the upstairs bathroom. Elizabeth indicated that she was allowed downstairs out of her locked room more than some of the other children because she would baby-sit and help her dad out. Elizabeth indicated that supper would not be served until her father returned home, usually around 6:00pm. Elizabeth indicated that supper would consist of sandwiches or sometimes something hot like a hamburger. Elizabeth also confirmed that the locks were changed on the doors on the Monday before her father went to California. Elizabeth indicated on the positive side regarding her father that he feeds them "good" and sometimes "sneaks" them treats. Elizabeth also indicated that her father sometimes talks her mother into letting them come downstairs for awhile, at which time they are allowed to come down and sit in a line in the kitchen area. Elizabeth indicated that if they began to make too much noise "mom gets mad" and they all have to go back into their rooms. Elizabeth also indicated that she has no real friends and is not allowed to have any visitors at the house. With respect to discipline, Elizabeth indicated that it is primarily administered by her father at her mother's direction. Elizabeth indicated that she has observed her father hit with a metal spoon, a strap, a pancake flipper, his fist, a hanger, and a bath brush. Elizabeth confirmed that a few weeks prior to September 22, 1987 her father struck Lisa with a brown strap because she stuck her head out the window. Elizabeth indicated that none of them are allowed to even look out the window and that if they do, they are punished. Elizabeth indicated that she recalls an incident from April or May,

Escape from the Dungeon

1987 when some Pepperidge Farm cookies were supposedly missing, causing her mother to become very angry. Elizabeth indicated that her mother got them all together and began hitting Jeffery with a flipper in order to elicit a confession about the missing cookies. Elizabeth recalls Holly confessing this at which time Ted, Jennifer, Holly, and Elizabeth were ordered to stand outside as their punishment. Elizabeth also informed your complainant that there had been a family outing in early August 1987, to Alpine Valley for the Madonna concert, at which time Michael, Lisa and Mary were left behind locked in two separate rooms. (Every once in a while, mom would take a couple of kids on an event. I never knew why she did this. In this case she took a couple of us to the Madonna concert. Not because it was something for the kids, but rather mom wanted to go and she took some of her pawns with her. She would use it to hold over our heads for months and months, over and over to get leverage. It was awful and often provided some of the worst memories and this time was no different. Many of the kids paid a big price that day.) *Elizabeth indicated that the baby, Jeffery, was left in his crib in the laundry room at this time also. Elizabeth indicated that the other family members were gone from the home about 2:00pm until midnight and that the kids diapers were "soaking wet" Elizabeth indicated that the children were given a sandwich at that time. Upon discussing meals times with Elizabeth, advised your complainant that she sometimes gets hunger pains because of missing meals or because of long time spans between meals. Elizabeth indicated that when she gets these pains, she lies down on the bed to ease the pain.*

Your complainant has further had occasion to speak with male juvenile Chip Stephens believed in this instance to be truthful and reliable who advised that on September 21, 1987 the day prior to being removed from the home, he stayed home from school because his mother was mad about something. Chip indicated that they were not given breakfast that morning and that they spent all day in their rooms. Chip recalled that this father changed the locks on two of the bedroom doors because his parents thought that some social workers might come to the home because of something Jennifer may have said while at Pathfinders. Chip further indicated that his parents had put duct tape on the doors so that they could tell if the children had come out of their rooms. Chip recalled that Andie had served them lunch on that day at about 3:00pm which consisted of peanut butter sandwiches. Chip recalled that Holly and Elizabeth were in their room that day with duct tape on the door and that Mary and Lisa were locked in their room all day also. Chip further indicated that they did not have any supper that evening, and he though that they were allowed out of their rooms about 10:20 pm to go to the bathroom. Chip indicated that for the past few years, his father has been sleeping on the floor in the upstairs hallway. Chip further indicated that he goes cleaning with his father and that while working, his father sometimes gives them special treats such as George Webb hamburgers. Chip admitted that he has taken small amounts of money from places they clean which he uses to buy food at school. Chip further indicated that his father does most of the cooking and laundry at home and that he has never seen his mother change the baby's diaper as the other children take care of the babies. Chip also described the Madonna concert outing and also confirmed that Michael, Lisa, Mary, and Jeffery were left behind locked in their respective rooms at home. Chip recalled that the family left for the concert at about 3:00pm and returned home sometime after midnight. Chip indicated that while they were away the four remaining children were not allowed to go to the bathroom and had no food but were fed a sandwich when the rest of the family returned home. Chip further recalled an incident from 1983 involving Ted being punished for going to the Super America station to get some gum and for letting their dog loose. Chip recalled that Ted's punishment involved being taken into the basement and tied to a support beam with the cord from the dehumidifier. Chip also described that Ted was stripped down to his underwear at this time and that his hands were tied behind his back. Chip indicated that all of the other children were then made to come down into the *basement and watch as mother began to hit Ted. Chip indicated that his mother said that, "this is what happens when you are bad". Chip indicated that Ted was then left in the basement. Chip indicated that he has also been hit in the past by his father and that his father has used a belt, a bath brush, and a steel hanger to do so. Chip also recalled the incident when his mother gathered them all together and made them watch her spank the baby, Jeffery. Chip's recollection was that the incident occurred because of $20 was missing. Chip further related that his mother was very protective of food and that she keeps inventory of what she buys using cash register receipts. Chip indicated that if any food was found to be missing, his mother would get very angry and attempt to find out who had eaten it. Chip further indicted that he felt this to be the reason why his mother keeps them all locked up. With respect to bathroom privileges, Chip also confirmed being locked in their rooms having to knock to get someone's attention, and hoping that someone would let them out to go to the bathroom. Chip indicated that if they were not let out they would try to hold it, but if they couldn't they would go to the bathroom in a bag in the room. Chip indicated that if he got caught doing this, his father would hit him with a belt. Chip also confirmed that no lights were permitted in his room except for a television set that was on most of the time. Chip said that the windows in his bedroom were nailed shut and that there were no air conditioners. Chip indicated that in the summer, it would get so very hot that they would sleep with their noses to the crack at the bottom of the door to get fresh air. Chip indicated that if they looked out a window, they would be punished for doing so. When asked about birthdays, Chip stated that usually there was a birthday cake at each of the kids' birthdays; however, Chip remembers one birthday were he was presented a homemade candle stuck in a cheerio.* (Chip had a rough childhood. Mom really belittled him and consistently joked about his birthday. She gave him a cheerio for a birthday cake and laughed in his face while having us watch. She really enjoyed belittling her children in front of everyone and had a sick sense of humor.)

Your complainant has further had occasion to speak with male juvenile Roger Stephens believed in this instance to be truthful and reliable, who confirmed many of the things previously told to your complainant by this older brothers and sisters, including being locked in their rooms and being let out in the mornings to get dressed for school. Roger indicated that piles of clothing were kept in the hallway and that his father usually made them breakfast which consisted of some kind of sandwich and milk which was then eaten in the upstairs bathroom. Roger indicated that when he returned home from school, he had to go directly to his bedroom and was locked in. Roger recalled incidents when he had knocked on his bedroom door to get out or to go to the bathroom. Roger indicated that if no one let him out, he would have accidents on occasion where he would go to the bathroom in his pants or in a bag. Roger indicated that one time this past summer when he had to go in a bag, his father hit him with a strap. Roger also recalled an incident when Ricky was strapped on his legs for pounding on the door because he had to go to the bathroom so bad. Roger indicated that his parents got mad at Ricky that time for making too much noise. Roger verified his attendance at the Madonna concert and also the fact that the younger children were required to remain home by themselves. Roger also indicated to your complainant that he was very much likes living in his new foster home where he had been for two days at the time of his interview with your complainant, further indicating that he likes the food and being able to play. (The boys received a lot a physical abuse. Each reacted differently. I remember Roger pounding his head on the wall nonstop in response to the abuse. He would just sit on the floor and keep hitting his head on the wall and make holes in the wall with his head. Roger was deeply affected by our upbringing and just like me, will need years before he can come to terms with his past. I am sure he doesn't even remember some of the things which happened. Like so many of us who blocked out so much of the bad, because it is just too hard to deal with and our minds are just protecting us from the past.)

Escape from the Dungeon

Your complainant, has further had the occasion to speak with male juvenile Ricky Stephens believed in this instance to be truthful and reliable who described his home life with his mother and father as "boring". Ricky indicated that he is also locked in his room and is only let out to eat or go to the bathroom. Ricky indicated that on school days he is let out of his room, gets dressed, and is fed a breakfast consisting of butter, jelly, peanut butter, or ketchup sandwich and some water or milk. Ricky indicated that they are given supper sometime between 8:00pm and 10:00pm and that they can go the bathroom at the same time. Ricky confirmed that when he is caught in this room going to the bathroom, he is strapped by his father. Ricky also recalled one incident where he missed a meal for some reason and was very hungry at the next meal. Ricky indicated that when he asked for more food, his dad hit him on the legs with a hanger. (This is so interesting because, evidenced by this 1987 statement, Ricky knows what went on in that house; however, in his 2004 statement he stuck to his story that "it wasn't that bad". It is sad to see. I figure that one of two things can explain this: either he has not and will not come to terms with what happened and the effect on him to this day or, he is merely protecting dad in this process. Ricky was clearly a central victim of mom's wrath and it saddens me that he hasn't come to terms with it. However, I am very empathetic to the fact that every child has to deal with this in their own way. In this case, Ricky's defense mechanism is to minimize the abuse and its' effects in order protect himself. I cannot in good conscience deny him this process. This is a very personal healing process and all I can do is try and understand why he does the things he does. I do not call him on it, I do not ask why he minimizes the situation nor do I ask him to confront the demons. It is his way of protecting himself and I cannot take that away from him. I can only hope and pray that he finds solace in his decisions and hope that he for his part can see why I do things the way I do them).

Your complainant has further had occasion to speak with female juvenile Suzy Stephens, believed in this instance to be truthful and reliable, who indicated that she did not like it at home because they eat meals at the wrong times. Suzy indicated that she likes staying at her foster home because she gets good things to eat that she has never had before. Suzy indicated that sometimes she would not be fed at home because her mother would be mad at someone. Suzy indicated that in the morning, the children are let out of their rooms to get dressed for school and that they got their clothes from piles in the hallway. Suzy indicated that sometimes she would not be given breakfast. Suzy indicated that she goes to school and upon her return home; she has to go up to her room where she is locked in. Suzy indicated that she shares this room with Lisa and Mary who are usually already locked in the room when she gets home from school. Suzy indicated that they stay in the room all night long and are given supper later in the night. She indicated that it is at this time that they are also allowed to use the bathroom. Suzy indicated that supper usually consists of a sandwich eaten in the bathroom and that she sees her mom only briefly in the morning before and after school. Suzy indicated that they do not have lamps in the rooms nor are they permitted to look outside. Suzy indicated that they do have television sets in their rooms. Suzy also said that the children do not have pajamas and that sleep in their clothing. Suzy also related that one time she was hit by her dad with a strap about four times for looking out the window. Suzy also indicated that she has been hit by her dad with his hand and with a bath brush. Suzy indicated that the time she was hit with the bath brush, she was struck in the stomach. Suzy related that she can have no visitors at the home and is not allowed to go to anyone's home and that she must come directly home from school. Suzy indicated that sometimes her mom yells at her and calls her a "little bitch". When asked about things she likes at her foster home, Suzy responded that she likes the fact that she can use the bathroom whenever she wants to, that she gets good food, and that she is not locked up, and that she can play outside. (Suzy was hit hard in the face with her past. To this day, she struggles with esteem and self worth and it tears me apart. In my opinion some of the kids have dealt with it well, while others have just let it go or simply pushed the situation aside. The kids that struggle with it, cause me the greatest heartache and continue to fuel my resentment towards my mother. The years and years of tearing Suzy down have left her in a state of self-destruction and feelings of no self worth or confidence. Suzy has tried several times to climb out of her personal dungeon of memories and despair and sometimes she comes out of it for a while other times she falls back in that bottomless pit. But the thing I applaud her for the most, is that she is still trying and still fighting to get out of it. Sooner or later when you keep fighting the fight you may win a battle or two. She is years behind right now but hopefully as the years progress she will take more steps forward than backward. I wish to God that I could just jump out and help so there is no pain for the individual child, but I know it is an impossible dream. It is tough to just sit by and not jump in and help change their world. About the only thing I can do is set an example for her and everyone else. Learning to live and work with the past that we had is about the best we can hope for).

Your complainant has further had occasion to speak with male juvenile Michael Stephens believed in this instance to be truthful and reliable, who also confirmed many of the things told to your complainant by the other children. Michael indicated that he attends kindergarten at Hoover School and goes for one-half day. Michael indicated that he shares his bedroom with Roger and Ricky and that he previously also shared it with Ted before Ted left home. Michael indicated that when he gets home from school, he gets a sandwich and sometimes gets to stay downstairs in the family room with Andie and

his mom and watch television. Michael indicated that when the other children got home from school, he would have to go upstairs with them and be locked in his room. He indicated that they would stay locked up until about 8:00pm when they would be let out for supper and to go to the bathroom. Michael recalled being left at home locked in his room when the family went to the Madonna concert, further indicating they left "when golf came on". Michael thought that they returned that night at about 2:00am at which time he was given some milk and a cheese sandwich. Michael indicated that prior to that he had been given only a peanut butter sandwich for breakfast the preceding morning. Michael indicated that he is happy living in the foster home because he gets good food and gets to play with toys.
(Michael is such an inspiration for me. He was so headstrong as a child that he often fought back to survive mom's tyranny. He has built up such a toughness that he has truly convinced me of his strength for the long haul in life. Michael was such a frail child that at first glance you would think he would not be able to defend himself, but he can hold his own like no other and I am so proud of him and his accomplishments after facing these issues. In this statement I think he was only 6 or 7 years old and to read this and know the man he has become brings tears to my eyes.)

Your complainant has further had occasion to speak with female juvenile Andie Stephens believed in this instance to be truthful and reliable who told your complainant that she gets to stay downstairs with Mom and Jeffery. Andie indicated that during the day, she and her mom go shopping and leave the young ones at home. Andie indicated that she would be with Mom and Dad sometimes when the other children were cleaning at night. Andie indicated that her dad sometimes hits her brothers and sisters with his hand or a belt and that she also recalls a recent incident in which money was missing. Andie indicated that Jeffery and Mary were hit by her dad so the others would tell who took the money. Andie also recalled that her dad had hit her on the legs with his hand and that it hurt. After speaking with Andie and the other children, your complainant was left with the impression that Andie may have received special treatment as "mom's favorite" which resulted in her being left out of the locked room more often that the other children. (Andie was much like Michael, and she too has survived the storm with a great deal of poise and dignity. Andie was about 4 or 5 here in these statements and spent the next 15 to 17 years really coming into her own. Andie has a strength and drive about her that surely came from the survival techniques she acquired in these years. Andie has no fear of telling any person on earth what she thinks and I think it is so admirable to have that type of confidence and air.)

5. Doctor's Statements

Your complainant has further reviewed a medical report submitted by Dr. Gerald Deutsch, believed in this instance to be truthful and reliable, who practice pediatric medicine in the Waukesha area. Dr. Deutsch's report indicates having occasion to examine all of the aforementioned Stephens children, with the exception of Ted. With respect to Jennifer, the only remarkable notes of his examination is that her right eyes vision is 20/30 and that her left yes is 20/40. With respect to Holly, her right and left eye vision is 20/70. With respect to Elizabeth her right and left eye vision is 20/30. With respect to Chip, Dr. Deutsch noted that Chip had complained of being frequently thrown from his bed by his father for being difficult to awaken to go to work in the cleaning business. Chip also related to Dr. Deutsch that he had some teeth chipped from being punched in the face by his father... Dr. Deutsch noted a cap on Chip's upper right front incisor and did observe a chip Chip's upper left front incisor. Chip was also found to be well below the 5th percentile regarding normal height for his age and below the 10th percentile regarding normal weight. Chip's vision was 20/40 in both eyes. With respect to Roger, Dr. Deutsch noted that Roger also complained of being punched in the mouth two years ago by his father *for wetting the bed. Dr Deutsch confirmed that he did observe a partially chipped tooth on Roger's bottom jaw. Dr. Deutsch also noted that Roger is also well below the 5th percentile regarding normal height and weight. With respect to Ricky, Dr Deutsch noted he was found to be in the 5th percentile regarding normal height and weight and further noted that his bone development is markedly delayed. With respect to Suzy, Kr. Deutsch noted her vision to be 20/50. Her only other complaint regarding having pain in her left leg while running. With respect to Michael, Dr. Deutsch noted that he appeared to be thin and small for his age and placed him in the 5th percentile regarding normal height and weight. With respect to Lisa, Dr. Deutsch noted that she was found to bin in the 25th percentile for normal height and weight. With respect to Mary, Dr. Deutsch found her to be in the 75th percentile regarding height and in the 25th percentile regarding weight, finding her development generally slow. With respect to Jeffery, Dr. Deutsch also found his development to be slow which Dr. Deutsch speculated be related to poor stimulation. It was also noted that he had mild facial and diaper rashes. Dr. Deutsch noted in his examination of Andie that she appeared thin but otherwise normal. Dr. Deutsch also noted that all of the older children, with the exception of Roger and Michael who were not tested, seemed to have marked visual problems which he believed may be caused by poor nutrition. Dr. Deutsch concluded that he felt the children may have had inadequate nutrition, which is evidenced by their height problems, as well as low carotene levels.*

None of what the doctors found was surprising to any of us. Every child in the family needed glasses due to lack of stimulation in the eyes. Because we were kept in our rooms with nothing but a black and white TV, our eyes paid the price. Every child had been malnourished and ill affected by lack of food in their height and weight. Every child was emancipated to the point that we would compare whose stomach sunk into our ribs the most. Everyone had dental issues beyond compare. Mom would use the excuse that bad teeth were genetic in our family and that we were all born without second enamels on our teeth. She would use that story with doctors non-stop. What she didn't tell the doctors is that we weren't allowed to brush our teeth and that toothpaste was a rare luxury if were allowed to have it. Schooling and academics was secondary to our life in the prison cells and took its toll in every developmental area.

6. Neighbor Statements

Officer Fischer's report further indicates speaking with several of he Stephens neighbors who also reside on Burdick Court, a cul-de-sac, in New Berlin. Officer Fischer indicates speaking with ordinary citizens George and Nancy Kriske, believed in this instance to be truthful and reliable, who advised that they have lived in their present residence since April 1987. The Kriskes advised that they are familiar with the Stephens family and felt that they kept strange hours. They also indicated that the never saw anyone outside. George Kriske indicated that he would see the older children come home at about 7:00 am when he was going to work. He also indicated that he believed the Stephens family had a summer home because they were never outside. The Kriskes further indicated that they saw the Stephens children outside about three times this entire past summer. They further indicated that the children seen outside at one time were about five.

Officer Fischer's report also indicates speaking with a former neighbor, ordinary citizen Christine Martin, believed in this instance to be truthful and reliable who advised that she lived next door to the Stephens family form April 1984 to December 1986. Mrs. Martin described the Stephens as being secretive people who she only saw when there were working in the yard or coming and going from the house. She indicated that she had some concerns about them because she didn't see the children outside except when they went to school. Mrs. Martin indicated that she had seen the Stephen's leaving between 1:30-2:00 am and that she would see 2-3 kids get out of the car at 6:30-6:45 am in the company of their father.

Officer Fischer's report also indicates speaking with another neighbor ordinary citizen Carleen Scale, believed in this instance to be truthful and reliable, who related that she is familiar with the location of the Stephens residence but that she never saw children playing there. Mrs. Scale indicated that she believed there were three children in the house. Mrs. Scale indicated that she noticed that of the numbers items in their yard, nothing ever seemed to have been used. Mrs. Scale particularly indicated that even with the hot summer this past season, she never saw anyone in the pool. Mrs. Scale described the Stephens home as being "like a haunted house" since she never saw anyone.

(Our neighbors, believe it or not, I cannot blame for not turning in our mother for abuse. It is amazing to know that none of the neighbors knew how many kids were in the house. Mom did a great job of keeping us so tightly behind closed doors that the neighbors never knew how many kids were in the house. There was a lot of shock when this story broke in 1987 and the neighbors just said that "they never knew" what was happening there. I think they were even distraught that they didn't know or felt they should have known and didn't do something. I often reflected on this strange truth. Isn't it sad that something so tragic can happen in the house next door with so many adults surrounding the home? I can only imagine what would have happened if someone did see something and someone had turned her in, how would life be different? In all actuality, I am not sure if I want to picture that. It is scary to know that one person can make such a difference if they truly want to. It is even scarier to think that some suspected something but did nothing to change it.)

7. *Parent Statements:*

This complaint is further based upon review of the written report of Cecil Roman of the Department of Human Services regarding notations she made as a result of a joint interview conducted with both defendants, Thomas and Linda Stephens, on September 29. 1987. Ms. Roman indicates that at the beginning of the interview that she and Marilyn Kraus verbally went through the Acknowledgement of Rights form with both defendants, and they were further permitted to converse with their attorney via telephone. Both defendants further indicated their willingness to discuss the situation with Ms. Roman and Ms. Kraus. Ms. Roman's report indicates that both Mr. and Mrs. Stephens acknowledge that at times when he would be outside the home or at bedtime or nap-time, the children would be locked in their rooms. They indicated that the majority of the time, however, it would be the boys who were locked in their rooms. Mrs. Stephens indicated that the house rule was that when any child was upstairs in their room, the door would be locked. Mrs. Stephens also acknowledged that the shades in the home were always pulled down but she had no explanation for this other than that she was a "night person." With respect to their cleaning business, both defendants explained that they started the business 20 years ago and that rather than hiring a babysitter at those odd hours, they got into the pattern of taking the children along on the jobs ever since the older children were babies. They indicated that they worked seven nights a week and that their usual start time was between 1:00am and 3:30 am. The defendants further indicated that Ted, Jennifer, Holly and Chip were the ones who would help with the cleaning business. Mrs. Stephens commented that she herself was appalled when she went upstairs after the children were removed form the residence. She acknowledged that she did not often go upstairs (mom hardly ever came upstairs – she made the family room her bedroom and lived down there) *and thought that she had last been upstairs about four weeks prior to the removal of the children. Mrs. Stephens indicated that she normally slept on a couch in the family room due to a back injury sustained in a car accident.* (This is a complete and utter fabrication in my opinion. She wasn't in a car accident nor had a back injury that was merely a sympathy card she played. One of many, I might add. She often would make up grandiose, bizarre stories in order to gain sympathy from those around her. Her reason for not coming upstairs was that she was so heavy that she couldn't climb the stairs and staying in the living room was easier). *Mrs. Stephens also acknowledged that there were locks on all the bedroom doors to "respect their children's privacy" and that they had been changed about a week or two before the children were removed from the residence. In reference to meals and where they were served, Mrs. Stephens acknowledged that it was routine for the children to eat in the upstairs bathroom. She was at a loss to explain how this pattern evolved other than to state it began by giving them a snack in the upstairs bathroom. Mrs. Stephens also admitted knowing that the children had been fed a diet consisting of mostly sandwiches. In reference to the children's limited bathroom privileges, both defendants stated that when the children called to use the bathroom, they would be allowed to do so. However, the defendants also acknowledged having found feces in the bedrooms. Mrs. Stephens indicated that the accidents in the bedrooms perhaps occurred if the older girls were home and did not hear the other children calling to use the bathroom. Mr. Stephens acknowledged the incident of September 17, 1987 in which Suzy reported to him that Lisa was in danger of falling out an open window and he recalls hitting Lisa two times on her buttocks with a strap. Both defendants acknowledged that Lisa sustained a red mark above the diaper line as a result of this. With respect to the incident of Jeffery being used to elicit information form the older children, Mrs. Stephens admitted that there had been some money missing, that she did have Jeffery on her lap, and that the four older children were present. Mrs. Stephens denied, however, actually hitting Jeffery, indicating that she was only going through the motions and was only hitting her own hand. Mrs. Stephens does not remember if Jeffery was crying at this time. With respect to the*

Madonna concert, the defendants disagreed as to which children actually went along. Mrs. Stephens believed that Michael had also gone to the concert. When questioned about who was left to supervise Jeffery and Lisa, Mrs. Stephens offered that her parents were in town from Michigan but was very evasive as to exactly where they were. (Mom used everyone in her life as a pawn including her own parents. Grandpa and Grandma Kanauz lived in Michigan at this time but mom often would lie and say they lived down the street or were close by in order to mitigate the seriousness of the charges. Every kid knew she lied about it.) *Upon being told that Ms. Roman the children had been left alone unsupervised, Mrs. Stephens remarked that she could not remember.*

Based on the foregoing, the complainant believed this complaint to be true and correct.

Philip Kiedrowski

Unfortunately then came the plea bargain and the following was an amended criminal complaint filed on April 6, 1988 against Mom and Dad:

Kathryn W. Foster, Assistant District Attorney for Waukesha County, Wisconsin being first duly sworn on oath, upon information and belief, says that: Between October 29, 1981 and September 22, 1987 in New Berlin, WI the defendants did:

    Count #1 *—being concerned wit the commission of the crime in that they did intentionally aid and abet the commission of said crime contrary to Wisconsin State Statutes, by acts and failure to act, contribute to the neglect of children to wit: Ted Stephens, Jennifer Stephens, Holly Stephens.*

And further advising the court that the above alleged offense is defined as a Class A misdemeanor and upon conviction of the above *alleged offense, the above named defendant is subject of a monetary fine of not more than $10,000 or imprisonment of not more than 9 months or both.*

Count #2–*Between October 29, 1981 and September 22, 1987, being concerned wit the commission of the crime in that they did intentionally aid and abet the commission of said crime contrary to Wisconsin State Statutes, by acts and failure to act, contribute to the neglect of children to wit: Elizabeth Stephens, Chip Stephens, Roger Stephens.*

And further advising the court that the above alleged offense is defined as a Class A misdemeanor and upon conviction of the above alleged offense, the above named defendant is subject of a monetary fine of not more than $10,000 or imprisonment of not more than 9 months or both.

Count #3– *Between November 2, 1981 and September 22, 1987, being concerned wit the commission of the crime in that they did intentionally aid and abet the commission of said crime contrary to Wisconsin State Statutes, by acts and failure to act, contribute to the neglect of children to wit: Ricky Stephens, Suzy Stephens, and Michael Stephens.*

And further advising the court that the above alleged offense is defined as a Class A misdemeanor and upon conviction of the above alleged offense, the above named defendant is subject of a monetary fine of not more than $10,000 or imprisonment of not more than 9 months or both.

Count #4– *Between July 23, 1985 and September 22, 1987, being concerned wit the commission of the crime in that they did intentionally aid and abet the commission of said crime contrary to Wisconsin State Statutes, by acts and failure to act, contribute to* *the neglect of children to wit: Andie Stephens, Lisa Stephens and Mary Stephens*

And further advising the court that the above alleged offense is defined as a Class A misdemeanor and upon conviction of the above alleged offense, the above named defendant is subject of a monetary fine of not more than $10,000 or imprisonment of not more than 9 months or both.

Count #5 *– Between December 27, 1986 and September 22, 1987, being concerned wit the commission of the crime in that they did intentionally aid and abet the commission of said crime contrary to Wisconsin State Statutes, by acts and failure to act, contribute to the neglect of children to wit: Jeffery Stephens.*

And further advising the court that the above alleged offense is defined as a Class A misdemeanor and upon conviction of the above alleged offense, the above named defendant is subject of a monetary fine of not more than $10,000 or imprisonment of not more than 9 months or both.

And prays that the defendant be dealt with according to law; that the basis for complainant's charge of such offense is: complainants review of the investigative reports of Investigator Philip Kiedrowski, Officer John Fischer, Sergeant William Miller, Officer Mark Hurst, Corporal Daniel Noordyk, and Officer Michael Jeannotte of the City of New Berlin Police Department, and Waukesha County Department of Human Services employees Cecil Roman and Marilyn Kraus, all believed in this instance to be truthful and reliable. Officer Fischer's report indicates all of the same facts reported in the report with counts #1-#13.

The entire incident from 1987 seems to be bizarre in so many different ways. Mom was able to explain away everything she was charged with and she is so manipulating and convincing that she got away with it.

She spun a tale of remorse and hope for change in the future. She spun the tale the authorities wanted to hear. They didn't know her though. They didn't realize that "they" were her pawns too. By begging for mercy and crying the story of how things were going to change, she was able to gain the sympathy (yes sympathy) of those that could have saved us. How can I blame them though? They didn't know her like we did. She was a monster.... an evil, conniving and manipulating monster whose strength only increased after she was able to manipulate the law enforcement agencies sent to protect us from her.

In a 1988 news paper article in the Milwaukee Journal by Darryl Enriquez he writes:

After approving a lengthy plan that gradually could return custody of 11 children to their New Berlin parents, Children's court Judge James Kieffer said Thursday that he feared that the abused youths might someday become abusive parents. In the Children's Court hearing Thursday, Kieffer said he was confused by how parents could treat their children as had been detailed in the petitions. He is a father of two. "I have an understanding of your background in that physical and emotional abuse may have been perpetrated on you, and you in turn perpetrated that on your children," Kieffer said. "I hope that when they become parents they will have learned from this experience. I hope they can lead productive lives." Kieffer said he viewed many hours of videotaped interviews of the children about what had happened in their home and found all of their stores consistent. "Shocked, dismayed and outraged, I was personally as a parent to learn what was going on in your household for years and years," he said.

Basically, my mother got off every single charge. Waukesha County social services gave all of the children back to my parents before the criminal procedures were done. Once mom got the kids back, she had immediate control over them again and manipulated every child into recanting their story. She had that much fear instilled into us. The system failed and allowed the manipulating contact between my mother and her children. She was able to convince them that life would be different if they only recanted their stories. She wined and dined them into submission to save her own hide. It is so sad to see in hind sight that the kids served as her pawns to save her hide. She did not care for the kids' health and welfare. She merely tried to save her own skin. The kids however, wanting so much to believe that their mother loved them, believed her. They recanted their stories, were returned to her home and walked right into the next level of abuse. Mom had no fear of the authorities and felt she lived at a higher level of society for getting off such serious charges. There is no way on God's green earth I can hold those kids accountable for the failing of the case so many years ago.

You would think after coming so close to going to jail that mom would have been deterred or learned her lesson, but she didn't. After the kids recanted their stories mom withdrew her Alfred Plea (which is the plea of no contest where she doesn't proclaim guilt or innocence) and the case went no further. The devastation to the children lasted nearly another two decades, as you will see the story unfold yet again.

Chapter 3

1988 – 2005

1989 – Car repossession incident – You would think I had learned from the first 19 years of my life not to trust mom, but I didn't. I fell into her trap over and over and this was the incident that led me to break the ties forever, or so I thought at the time. In 1989 I bought a shiny red new convertible. Somehow, someway I was able to get a car loan and had this over the top great and wonderful vehicle to drive around in. I am not sure what possessed me to get it, I am sure it had a lot to do with the fact that I was 19 years old and overcompensating for things I never had in my years growing up. Over the next year, I underestimated my ability to pay for the car and my mother sweet talked me. Yes, she sweet talked me yet again with her manipulating ways and made me believe she would take care of her oldest daughter and look out for her financial status. It was my own fault. I should have taken responsibility for my failures, but I didn't. Mom insisted she would take the car "off my hands" and she said she would pay all of the payments, but I would have to give her the car. A long story made short, the payments were never made and the car was repossessed in my name. I spent the next eight years recovering from that error in judgment. I had so much anger for her because my credit was ruined, but I had only myself to blame. I should have known better. I slipped back into her control for a minute and it ruined me for a decade. . In hind sight I am glad this happened because it continued to shape me for the person I am today. I stayed away for the next two years and tended to my own life.

1989 – One of the most distinct memories I have was when I was living in Wauwatosa, WI. I found myself going to church. I remember sitting in the pews during mass with tears in my eyes and praying to God as the priest walked by. I remember saying in my head, "God please let them see how hurt I am. Please God let the priest offer to help me." This happened week in and week out. I thought if I prayed enough and if I hurt enough that the priests would see it in my eyes and help me out of my own personal hell. But the weeks went by and tears wept from my eyes. I was so alone. No family, no friends, it was just me and my conversations with God. I had my best friend Meg and there was also Ted, but I felt all alone in my suffering. Maybe I didn't want to bring them into my painful life, maybe I didn't want to burden them anymore than I already had. Sometimes I think I was ashamed and embarrassed for everything that happened. Whatever my reasons for not allowing myself to see my friend that stood before me, I felt alone. Alone to live in pain and just didn't want to bring Meg into this side of my life. In fact, as she had read this story for the first time I think she is first getting the understanding of the level of pain and anguish that I was facing back then. With each story and each remembrance, we become closer friends and I appreciate her more today than any other time in my life. Back then, I remember deciding that if they couldn't see the terror that I was living in, then it must not be a bad enough situation and that others needed them more than I did. So I marched on. Yet, I wanted so badly to get confirmed into the Catholic faith, but I was riddled with guilt. The one thing that always plagued me with guilt after I left in 1987 was those kids in the house by themselves. I pictured them there while I was free of her. My heart sank every time I thought of mom in one of her rages and pulling out the old "bug eyes" she was so famous for. I would cry at night to think those babies were crying in their rooms. For three or four years, there was incredible guilt and when mom got off the charges my heart sank. I just wanted to take all of the kids with me. I made an appointment with the priest from the church at the end of the block and I asked him, how can I be a good Catholic when I can't live up to the Ten Commandments. How could I ever honor my mother and still be confirmed? He looked at me and I think he saw some of the pain, but I never told him about my whole childhood. I think he sensed it though, because he said that if the parents set a bad example and did bad things that the commandment did not apply to them. A great deal of relief swept over me that day and I enrolled in the confirmation classes. I went with the other adults to the weekly class, but then something happened that "forced" me to not go through with it. I had to have someone who was confirmed in the catholic faith to sponsor me. One slight problem, I had no one who fit that bill. I knew plenty of folks like Fr. Reiny and some other teachers at High School, but no one I would even consider talking to. I lived my life in a world of isolation, I didn't know how to ask for help, and even if I could ask, I am not sure how I would have accepted it. Even in my mid-thirties I find it hard to ask or accept help. I feel as if I am sometimes on a deserted island even though I know I have a friend to my left and right. It is a feeling of loneliness that can only be cured through time, healing and self-confidence built on esteem. I know the person I appear to be, but it isn't the person I feel like and it is a level of isolation that is sometimes incomprehensible to the "typical" person on the street. At that time in my life, I knew no one, had no family that I could turn to for things like this and did not want to ask a complete stranger to do this for me. I was so embarrassed that I left the class and never went back. I don't go to church much anymore, but when I go, I have such a sense of peace. It feels like I am forgiven for my cold heart towards my mother and for my wall that I have built around myself over the last 35 years that no one besides my children has been able to penetrate. In church it is just me and God, where there is nothing but unconditional love.

1991 – Mom called a press conference and manipulated us into participating – This press conference was called just seven months before I enlisted in the army, and most likely led me to that profession. She is the master manipulator and this woman conned us all over and over again. She talked her way out of felonies. She talked her way out of everything. I found this out years after the fact, but she contacted the paper and requested that a story be done on how she had brought her family back together. She didn't tell anything about the story to the kids, rather she said that the newspaper just wanted to do a family photo and that was it. Since I had removed myself from that life, I thought this would be my last opportunity to get a picture with my siblings so I agreed to sit for the photo. Little did I know, it was a set-up. Little did I know what the article would say. I was so lividly upset after that article that I just sank again to a bottomless pit. How many times am I going to go through this before I learn my lesson? That day, I decided no more, that woman would get no more trust, no more chances to manipulate me. She duped me for the last time.

Sep 1987 – 2004 – What happened over the next few months, I learned about years later when the second set of allegations surfaced in 2004. Generally all of us kids were put into foster homes. Most of us were separated, but some of the kids were placed together. We were shuffled from home to home until we all found some sort of permanency. One of my teachers at Pius agreed to take me in for my senior year, the Frohna's. How grateful I am to them for taking in someone they knew nothing about and who had quite the sorted past. My time with them was short, less than a year, but they got me graduated. They got me to some social events to show me what a normal teenager does. I got my drivers license and I went on my first date not governed by my mother. Meg was so important to me over that senior year. We did Forensics club together, we hung out at her house and I dated her cousin once or twice. Little did I know that this friend would be my friend for life and through both of our adventures across the world, we would always find comfort in each other and our conversations. After high school I managed to stay in college, although I had a six month phase where I fell in with the wrong crowd and lived the unsavory part of life... but I saw the light and stayed in college and worked three jobs. Even if I took one class at a time, I stayed in college. It was something for me to work for, a dream to make come true.

While I was in high school, my parents somehow, someway got off -- all the charges were dismissed and they got the kids back and with that, back in the house. I was so let down by the system. Perhaps worst of all, my mother succeeded in getting all of my brothers and sisters to hate me and turn their backs on me. So, I ran again. This time I ran to the Army. I have no idea to this day what made me walk into the recruiting office on Oakland Avenue that day, but it was a day that changed my life forever. When I went to the recruiter I had two years of college under my belt and was able to go in as a Private First Class (E-3) vs. a private (E-1). I was too scared to do active duty so I joined the Army Reserve to see what it would be like. As the next three years went by, I had my first long-term relationship and continued to go to college. The army had a commissioning program to make young enlisted people into officers. I wanted to make a better life for myself and my significant other so I went to Officer Candidate School at Fort Benning, GA and became a 2nd Lieutenant in the United States Army on Active Duty. Then the unbelievable, I got pregnant and my long time love for the last three years left my side. I was devastated again. How could I be a single mom in the military? I was assigned to Fort Knox, KY where I had the opportunity to show my worth as an officer and become used to being a single mom. I had a good Colonel in my chain of command. He looked out for me and afforded me the opportunity to go to school at night after duty hours. I worked so hard. I worked all day and went to school for 3 hours every night in Louisville. Well, I was a young single mom and I didn't qualify for assistance with child care or WIC programs (this is one of the reasons I want to be in Congress) so I had to take my daughter to school with me every night. I talked to my instructors and I said, "I am motivated and I am dedicated. I have to get a degree to make a better life for myself and my lovely daughter Sam so would you mind if I brought her to class every night? If she cries I will go in the hall." Those instructors at the University of Louisville said I was more dedicated than most of their traditional students and they afforded me a lot of latitude. In fact, when it came time to graduate from college, I again had no one. I had worked eight years for my degree and succeeded in spite of every land mine thrown in my way. It was 1997 and I was alone, but I wasn't going to miss my graduation from college. So, what did I do? Sam was two years old and she walked across the stage with me. The professors all clapped and they gave my daughter the diploma. I got a nice stranger to take our picture. What a memory, it brings tears to my eyes today just to think about it. I bought a class ring which was $300 I couldn't afford, but I took out a loan because that ring, which I wear to this day, is a sign of triumph. I am succeeding in spite of my mother.

Escape from the Dungeon

I gave up dating. Who would want to date a single mother with a history like mine? I had the word "baggage" written over the front of my forehead. So, I just gave up looking, but secretly hoped for that knight in shining armor to save me. I did occasionally go on a first date but not many second dates. I decided to focus on my career and my daughter, nothing else mattered. Then I got orders to go to Hawaii where mobilizations were commonplace. Somehow, someway I made it work and somehow, someway I impressed a commander with my work ethic because he gave me a job as the Boat Commander in Pearl Harbor where my area of responsibility was the Pacific Ocean. Wow... but somehow, someway I made it work... but I wanted to get back to Wisconsin and my family, my brothers and sisters that is.

Finally in 1991 I was sent to Fort Sheridan, IL and I bought a home in New Berlin just a mile away from the dungeon. To this day I cannot explain why I chose to live so close to the dungeon that I was able to escape from. Later in the book I describe Stockholm Syndrome where abused people tend to relate to their abusers. That is probably the best explanation. New Berlin is my home and I don't know why I find comfort here, but it is where I will live for the rest of my life. Many of the other kids live very close to home as well, probably for the same reasons In fact, in after the three year tour in Hawaii I got this job specifically so I could live in New Berlin and allow my daughter the opportunity to get to know her aunts, uncles and cousins. I even submitted to driving 1 ½ hours each way from Waukesha County, WI to Fort Sheridan, IL everyday just so I could provide that "family" type of environment to my daughter. Being in the military for so long makes you transient by nature and I wanted one place in the world that my daughter could call home and she knew she would be going back to after we finished with the military. I decided to treat this move back as a "test" to see if I could stomach living so close to this evil woman. It was with a great deal of skepticism that I took everything in. I constantly was paranoid of her deceptive ways and questioned every little thing that went wrong. Luckily for me, she left me alone and as soon as I had the chance I reconnected with all my siblings who had reached adulthood and were allowed to escape the dungeon. We had good times and bad and had family gatherings like Ted and I dreamed we would have when we were little. I gradually regained contact with each of the children as they left home, but I trusted no one and was on guard for years before I began to believe we could have a sibling relationship with one another. Slowly but surely, we started to become a family without Mom and Dad and for years that was great. We heard rumblings now and again that mom was out of control and several of the older siblings made complaints to the authorities, but nothing became of them. Mom sweet-talked her way out of it each time. Strangely, one day while I was at my sister-in-law's parent's house, which coincidently is down the block from the dungeon, I saw a pack of kids walking to Hoover for school. I asked my brother, "who are those kids?", and he told me they were our brothers and sisters. I was shocked. I couldn't recognize my own brothers and sisters on the street in front of me. I caught glimpses of them now and then but nothing significant. Then came March 23, 2004.....

March 23, 2004 – The day the kids were taken away... again!! – Another day in the history of our family that is difficult to forget. I received a call out of the blue from my sister Holly saying the youngest four kids whom I had never met or known before were taken away from mom. Jeffery, the oldest of the four, had turned my parents in for abuse. My jaw dropped down to the ground in disbelief, but more of relief. I immediately went to Holly's house where I found the kids sleeping in the living room. I walked in and said "Hi, I am your sister Jennifer. Boy am I glad to meet you guys!" Holly gave me a run down of what had happened. Much like myself at the very same age, Jeffery had had enough. He knew I had been emancipated and made a legal adult at the age of 17 so he went to his guidance counselor to see how he could do the very same thing. From then on, the police were involved. They took the four children from school and Holly took emergency custody of them. I spent that entire first day just sitting with my brothers and sister whom I had never met and just talked. I found out who they were and allowed them to meet me and know that I would be there for them. Over the course of the next few days, I became the permanent home for Nick who was 16 years old and a sophomore in High School and Jeffery who was 17 and a senior. We had a 17 and 18 year age gap between me and them. Charlie was diabetic. I could not care for him so he went to a foster home and Amber stayed with Holly.

As one might imagine, these weeks brought the nightmares to life all over again. Nick and Jeffery were thrown into a home with a sister they had never met and I was suddenly responsible for four kids as a single parent. My rules were strict and as the emotions played out, Nick shut down on me. He left my custody after a few short weeks and went to live with Ted for a few months before moving to a permanent foster home only a mile away from my house. Amber became too much for Holly and her five children so she came to live with me and through a barrage of emotional rollercoaster's and a stint at Elizabeth's house, Amber went to a loving foster home, also just a couple of miles from my house. Jeffery had a few rough spots but now lives in his own apartment after graduating from high school and loves it. He works full time at various jobs and is going through normal 18 year old stuff with responsibility and relationships. Today, the kids spend a lot of time at my house to give the foster parents a break and they are thriving beyond belief. We hope mom is held accountable for years to come so these last three children can be given the best chance possible to succeed.

As the investigation into these latest allegations rolled forward, so many other situations of illegal activity came to light along with more unsuspecting victims of her manipulations.

2004 - Mom's 1998 internet affair and manipulation of John Doe– One of the most surprising things that came out in the investigations in 2004 was that mom had an affair with a gentleman from Florida. To protect the identity of another innocent victim, I will not divulge the name of this gentleman, because if I were in his shoes, I too would want to forget the whole thing happened. Below is a reading of the criminal complaint filed against my mother Linda on August 9, 2004:

Count #1 – On August 15, 1998, at Great Midwest Bank, in Waukesha County Wisconsin, the defendant, Linda Stephens did: utter as genuine a bank check, then and there well knowing the same falsely purported to have been made by.... John Doe.... whereas in truth in fact the said John Doe did not give such authority.

And further advising the Court that the above alleged offense is defined as a Class C felony; upon conviction of the above alleged offense, the above named defendant is subject to a fine of not more than $10,000 or imprisonment of not more than ten years, or both.

Count #2 – On August 17, 1998 at

Escape from the Dungeon

Great Midwest Bank, in Waukesha County Wisconsin, the defendant, Linda Stephens did: utter as genuine a bank check, then and there well knowing the same falsely purported to have been made by.... John Doe.... whereas in truth in fact the said John Doe did not give such authority.

And further advising the Court that the above alleged offense is defined as a Class C felony; upon conviction of the above alleged offense, the above named defendant is subject to a fine of not more than $10,000 or imprisonment of not more than ten years, or both.

And prays that the defendant be dealt with according to law.; that the basis for complainant's charge of such offense is: based upon complainant's own investigation into these allegations while working with the City of New Berlin Police Department.

The detective in charge provided this report to these two counts:

Said reports indicate that, in March 2004, your complainant and other officers of the City of New Berlin Police Department executed a Search Warrant at the residence of Linda Stephens in the City of New Berlin. During the course of executing that Search Warrant, officers found several documents that provided information relative to checks being written on the account of John Doe to pay bills for Linda Stephens. In the course of his investigation, your affiant contacted John Doe, a common and ordinary citizen-victim, believed in this instance to be truthful, and John Doe reported that, back in 1998, some of his checks turned up missing, and there were numerous activities conducted on his account at Great Midwest Bank without his consent. Said reports further indicate that John Doe reported that in early 1998 he met with Linda Stephens through an Internet chat room, and they eventually established a relationship online. Eventually, John Doe came to move to Wisconsin, and Linda Stephens assisted him in locating an apartment. Linda Stephens represented herself as being 28 years of age and having 2 children. When John Doe met her in person, he found that she had misrepresented quite a few things about herself. In spite of that, John Doe and Linda Stephens maintained a friendship.

Said reports further indicate that John Doe reported that during the time he had a relationship with Linda Stephens, she asked him on a number of occasions to write checks for her to pay various bills. She promised him that she would reimburse him later; however, when she did reimburse him later, it was with personal checks that later were found to be on accounts that were closed or did not have sufficient funds. Also during the course of his relationship he discovered that his checkbook was missing and eventually learned that a number of checks had been issued without his consent. The checking account he was referring to was the checking account in his name at Great Midwest Bank.

Said reports further indicate that John Doe consented to bank records being released and your complainant viewed the bank record from his account at Great Midwest Bank. The record reflect that, starting on June 22, 1998, a series of checks began being deposited into John Doe's account drawn on an account under the name of Linda Stephens with Bank of America. That particular account was closed in December 1997 so no money ever made it to John Doe's account. On July 29, 1998 John Doe completed an Affidavit of Fraudulent Transaction at his bank regarding several automated teller machine withdrawals. John Doe said that he had never received his ATM card in the mail.

Said reports further indicate that your complainant interviewed several of the children of Linda Stephens, all of whom are common and ordinary citizens believed in this instance to be truthful, who reported that they had witnessed their mother taking mail from John Doe's mailbox. At the time John Doe filed the Affidavit of Fraudulent Transaction, the account with the fraudulent activity was closed and a new account was opened. Subsequent to that time, beginning on August 4, 1998, a number of additional deposits were made to John Doe's account without his knowledge. More than a half dozen deposits were made into John Doe's new account at Great Midwest Bank with personal checks drawn on the account of Linda Stephens through Bank of America. The account referenced on those checks could not be located. John Doe reviewed the deposit slips for those particular deposits and stated that he did not fill out those documents.

Said reports further indicate that the bank records reflected that shortly after the deposit were made to John Doe's account, someone began writing checks from John Doe's account at Great Midwest Bank was cashing in the amount of $870 at the Great Midwest Bank. The check was dated August 14, 1998 and issued to Linda Stephens. The check was signed by John Doe and the back of the check was endorsed by Linda Stephens. John Doe viewed the photocopy of that check and stated that he did not issue that check to Linda Stephens and reported that his signature on the front had been forged.

Said reports further indicate that all the way into September of 1998 there were a number of additional unauthorized deposits into John Doe's account and a number of additional forged checks cashed on his account. Because of the timing of deposits that turned out to be on closed or unfound accounts, relative to the timing of the forged checks being issued on the account, payments were made and John Doe's account ended up being overdrawn.

Said reports further indicate that your affiant reviewed the reports of Detective Loeding, of the City of Greenfield Police Department, Green field Wisconsin, a fellow law enforcement officer believed in this instance to be reliable. Detective Loeding became involved in investigating the fraudulent activity on John Doe's account back in 1998. During the course of that investigation, Linda Stephens admitted that she had conducted the fraudulent activity on John Doe's account. She claimed to have been his fiancée and promised that she would remedy the problem with the account being overdrawn.

Based on the foregoing, the complainant believes this complaint to be true and correct.

Ryan Park

Now this report in itself is completely amazing but not so shocking when you consider everything else mom has done.... but there is more to this story not covered here. Mom had spun a tail of deceit to this man to an unbelievable level. When she initially started talking to him she emailed a picture of her third oldest daughter, Elizabeth, and represented that she was her (my sister is very pretty and petite). She also told John Doe that her husband Tom, my Dad, was actually her brother living with her and that she used to be married to Ted (who is actually her oldest son and my oldest brother) who was a Navy Seal and died in action (Ted was in the Navy but was never a Seal and never died, of course). Mom never told him she had sixteen kids and I am just shocked that the sick mind of this woman portrayed her son as her husband. To my mind, this is just sick and perverted.

I had the opportunity one occasion at the court house for a preliminary hearing to meet this John Doe who seemed to be a perfectly normal guy. In my opinion, he was just some normal guy from Florida who got majorly duped over the internet and remains completely embarrassed by the entire event. I asked some pretty blunt questions and received answers which told me what I already knew to be true. I asked him how mom had explained the stark contrast between the pretty and petite young woman in the picture he received from her and her actual weighty self. And, how did she explain the fact that she had no teeth? He stated that Linda told him she had cancer and she was so convincing he believed her. To this day I cannot understand why my father allowed this to happen. How could he not have known? And if he did, why did he let this happen? Linda would take some of the younger children to the apartment she rented for John Doe where she would have physical relations with this man while the kids were in the living room. I can only imagine what was going through the minds of those brothers and sisters. I never did ask them. I just want to remain in ignorant bliss and hope they didn't realize what was going on under their noses.

2004 – Mom's actions following the death of her father – When I moved back to Wisconsin after spending ten years in the military, I had to deal with many of old issues I had left behind years ago. One of those was Grandpa Kanauz whom I had not seen since I was 8 or 9 years old. Well, as it turned out – when I moved back to New Berlin, I found that my Grandpa Kanauz lived in New Berlin and had taken a retirement job bagging groceries to keep him busy. I couldn't believe my eyes! There he was, the grandfather of my childhood whom I hadn't seen for nearly twenty-five years! I never saw my grandmother and I believe she had died a couple of years earlier from complications from diabetes and Grandpa Kanauz was trying to keep busy. When I got through the line, I looked at him and asked "do you know who I am?" (a question I have posed to many of my brothers and sisters as well). Grandpa was rather ecstatic and hugged me. He spoke up in a loud voice to all the cashiers on the line and told them that I was his oldest granddaughter. He asked me many things in that small moment of time and I was simply taken aback at this meeting. I told him I had joined the Army and was living back in town. We hugged and then he yelled again, "and she is a Captain in the Army". He seemed quite proud and grateful to meet even under the circumstances at hand. I think we just appreciated each other in that moment. I went to Pick 'n Save a lot over that year just to tell him a few stories. He would always say to the cashier, "That's my grand-daughter. She is an officer in the Army." Then something bad happened. Grandpa went to the store's annual Christmas party and while he was on the dance floor he fell over and had a fatal heart attack.. I wasn't very close to Grandpa so I didn't have a whole lot of emotions. Part of me feels incredibly guilty for that and I wish I would have had the time to really get to know him better. I will say though that I was sad for many of the children that did know him and their reactions. I didn't find out the rest of the story until a couple of days later. It horrified me and paints an exact picture of who my mother really is. How would any normal person react upon find out their father had died? Denial? Desperation? Maybe run to the hospital to see if it is really true, right? Well not Linda, her first response when she found out that her father had had a heart attack was not to rush to her father's side, but rather to ransack his apartment for valuables. She got in her car, used a key she had for his apartment in New Berlin and took every valuable he had including his car and credit cards. What a great daughter - and it gets worse. She used those credit cards for months to buy art, go on cruises and buy lots of items online.

Below is a reading of the criminal complaint filed against Linda on October 8, 2004 for these actions:

Count #1 – *On multiple occasions between December 10, 2001 and February 11, 2002 Linda Stephens did as a party to a crime, contrary to Wisconsin State Statutes did intentionally take and carry away movable property of another, to wit: Providian MasterCard, said property having a value greater than $2500,* *without the consent of said owner and with intent to deprive the owner permanently of possession of such property.*

And further advising the court that the above alleged offense is defined as a Class C felony; upon conviction of the above alleged offense, the above name defendant is subject to a fine of not more than $10,000 or imprisonment of not more than 15 years or both.

The most surprising fact here is that the penalty for "property removal" is so much higher than that of "cruel maltreatment of children". It is sad to say this is the case and is part of the reason I want to help make a difference on a legislative level. Right now in my opinion, there is not nearly enough accountability for actions like those inflicted onto children by their own parents. The repercussions are much too light in my eyes.

Count #2 *– On multiple occasions between December 10, 2001 and December 17, 2001 Linda Stephens did as a party to a crime, contrary to Wisconsin State Statutes did intentionally take and carry away movable property of another, to wit: JC Penny, said property having a value greater than $2500, without the consent of said owner and with intent to deprive the owner permanently of possession of such property.*

And further advising the court that the above alleged offense is defined as a Class C felony; upon conviction of the above alleged offense, the above name defendant is subject to a fine of not more than $10,000 or imprisonment of not more than 9 months or both.

And prays that the defendant be dealt with according to law; that the basis for complainant's charge of such offense is: based upon complainant's own investigation into these allegations while working with the City of New Berlin Police Department.

Said reports indicate that on March 26, 2004, officers from the New Berlin Police Department executed a search warrant at the residence of Linda Stephens in New Berlin. In the course of this search warrant, officers took into custody a large number of financial documents, and during the course of the financial documents, the discovered paperwork documenting a large volume of financial transactions on various accounts of John N. Kanauz, the deceased father of Linda Stephens. A detective obtained a death certificate from the Waukesha County Register of Deeds confirming that John N. Kanauz passed away on December 9, 2001. The detective checked with Waukesha County Register of Probated and determined that it appears that the estates of John and June Kanauz have never been probated.

Said reports further indicate that knowing that John N. Kanauz passed away on December 9, 2001, it struck detectives as odd that the financial documents they found all dealt with credit transactions conducted on John N. Kanauz's accounts after both he and his wife had passed away.

Said reports further indicated that what first alerted detectives to the problem was a letter in the possession of Linda Stephens, but addressed to John N. Kanauz from the Providian Financial Fraud Department. The letter was dated February 25, 2002 and indicated that Providian was investigation the unauthorized use of John Kanauz's credit card. The letter reflected that the card had been reported stolen on December 10, 2001 the day after John Kanauz passed away, and there were a large number of unauthorized charges made starting on December 10, 2001 through February 11, 2002. Charges totaled $46,876.55. Documentation reflected that the charge card was used on multiple occasions to obtain cash advances at locations on 108th St and 124th St in West Allis, to pay Verizon phone bills, to pay for groceries at Pick N Save in West Allis, to pay charges to Wisconsin Gas Company, to pay for Direct TV service, to make purchases from Dell Computers Catalog Sales, to make purchases from Sears.com, to make a purchase from the Sears store at Brookfield Square, to make seven charges to Celebrity Cruise Lines, to make seven airline ticket charges for tickets issued in the name of Linda Stephens to make a charge to Target.com and to make a charge to the Radisson Hotel in San Juan, Puerto Rico, to make a charge to APCOA/Standard Parking in Milwaukee, to make a charge to the Mirage Hotel in Las Vegas, and to make a charge to Link Systems, Inc., in Milwaukee.

Said reports further indicate that a detective contacted a representative of Providian Financial a common ordinary citizen believed in this instance to be truthful, who indicated that Providian Financial had made contact with Linda Stephens, since Linda was, in one way or another, the recipients of most, if not all of the charges made after John Kanauz's death. The representative from Providian Financial stated that Linda Stephens admitted that she had used the credit card and said that she would pay back all of the money owed to Providian. As of May 2004, no money has been paid on the account balance, which had risen to $47,305.82 by March 2002. Documents relating to the account reflected that shortly after the unauthorized charges began, payments were made to Providian Financial on nearly a daily basis. The amounts of the payments ranged from several hundred dollars to the highest payment of $19,145. Each of those payments was eventually reversed, however, it often took as long as two weeks for the reversal to be noted, thus, Providian Financial, on several occasions, would notify the cardholder, John Kanauz, whom they did not know payment would be received, therefore, additional charges would be authorized. Because payments kept coming in, it took some time before the fraud department was alerted.

Said reports further indicated that investigators subsequently started following up on some of the charges that were reported to be unauthorized. A detective spoke with a representative from Sears Corporation, who confirmed that multiple charges were made on the internet through Sears.com with payment being made by way of the

Providian MasterCard of John Kanauz. There was a charge on December 29, 2001, in the amount of $251.40 for a Kenmore garbage disposal and a Kenmore humidifier. The shipping address was Tom Stephens Cleaning, 12430 W. Burdick Ct, New Berlin, WI 53151. On January 4, 2002, separate credit transactions were made over the internet for Jenn-Air dishwasher and a Jenn-Air trash compactor, both of which were shipped to that same address in New Berlin, however, those two orders were both cancelled. There was a third order made on January 4, 2003, for a Frigidaire electric range in the amount of $1,014.51. That item shipped to the Burdick Court address. These charges matched up with balances reflected on John Kanauz's credit card statement and the February 25, 2002 letter to John Kanauz letter from Providian. When officers from the New Berlin Police Department executed a search warrant on the Stephens resident on Burdick Court on June 7, 2004, they found all three of the charged items at the Stephens residence.

Said reports further indicate that the representative from Sears stated that there was also an in store purchase on December 29, 2001, which was paid for with the Providian MasterCard of John Kanauz. A Kenmore water heater was purchased and was shipped to the Stephens residence. A detective subsequently checked and found that on January 4, 2002 the New Berlin Building Inspector issued a permit for installation of a water heater at the Stephens residence. The permit reflected that the water heater was to be installed by Water Tight Plumbing, which has a contract with Sears at Brookfield Square to install water heaters. The permit application and the job ledger were both in the name of John Kanauz, but the water heater was to be installed at the Stephens residence on Burdick Court. When officers executed a search warrant on June 7, 2004, at the Stephens residence, they found the fraudulently purchased water heater.

Said reports further indicate that a detective contacted a representative of Dell Computers and learned that two purchases were made on

December 20, 2001 which were both paid for with the Providian MasterCard of John Kanauz. While the charges were billed to John Kanauz, the items were all shipped to Tom TLS Cleaning Stephens, 12430 W. Burdick Court. These items also appeared on John Kanauz's billing statements. The first purchase was for a 4300S Dimension computer which cost $1,349.88. The second purchase was for a printer, some associated cables, a digital camera, a few other items which all totaled $720. The representative from Dell indicated that the credit card company charged these purchase back to Dell, therefore, Dell is seeking $2,093.64 in restitution. When officers executed the search warrant on June 7, 2004, they found the printer, printer cable, and computer in the Stephens residence.

Said reports further indicate that the detective followed up by contacting a representative of the Radisson Ambassador Plaza Hotel in San Juan, Puerto, a common ordinary citizen believed in this instance to be truthful. The representative reported that a hotel stay was booked for Linda Stephens, but was paid for with the Providian MasterCard of John Kanauz. Also on the account was a $300 cash advance from an automatic teller machine located in the Radisson Hotel.

Said reports further indicated that a detective spoke with a representative of Celebrity Cruises-Infinity, a common ordinary citizen believed in this instance to be truthful. A representative reported that the Providian MasterCard of John Kanauz was used to book a cruise for Linda at a cost of $3,433.70. Also, while on board during the cruise, Linda Stephens took cash advances totaling approximately $6,000 and Tom took cash advances totaling approximately $5,000 all billed to the Providian MasterCard of John Kanauz.

Said reports further indicate that the representative from Celebrity Cruises also reported that the Providian MasterCard of John Kanauz was also used to purchase numerous pieces of artwork from the Park West At Sea Auction House, which performed auctions on *the cruise. A detective subsequently spoke with a representative from park West At Sea Auction House, which performed auctions on the cruise. A detective subsequently spoke with a representative from Park West At Sea, a common ordinary citizen believed in this instance to be truthful, and learned that there were 12 pieces of artwork purchased by Linda Stephens using the Providian MasterCard of John Kanauz. She purchased approximately $34,000 in artwork, which included a single Picasso painting that they purchased for $26,430. All of the auction purchases took place between January 31, 2002 and February 3, 2002. They were able to carry one of the pieces of artwork off the ship. It was a print entitled, "Equine Dance II." All of the other items needed to be shipped from inventory, however, a fraud alert was reported before any of those items were actually shipped. Your complaint subsequently recovered "Equine Dance II" from a friend of Linda Stephens who reported that he had received that print as a gift from Linda Stephens. That individual is a common ordinary citizen believed in this instance to be truthful, who identified himself to police, however, he wishes not to be named in court documents.*

Said documents further indicate that a detective spoke with Investigator Kurt Roussell an employee of WE Energies, which was formally known as Wisconsin Gas Company. Mr. Roussell a common ordinary citizen believed in this instance to be truthful, was well familiar with the Linda Stephens account. He reported that between December 26, 2001 and February 25, 2002, Linda Stephens made 14 charges on their residential account that they paid for with the Providian MasterCard of John Kanauz. They used the card to build up an excess balance on their residential account in excess of $5,000. Then, on February 15, 2002, Linda Stephens contacted Wisconsin Gas Company and told a story about having built up the credit balance due to the fact that she and her husband were going to be leaving town for an extended period, however the plans to leave town were cancelled, therefore, she would like to obtain some of the excess balance in a refund. In the first call, Linda

Escape from the Dungeon

Stephens sought and subsequently received a refund check in the amount of $2,800. She subsequently contacted Wisconsin Natural Gas again and sought an additional $900 refund check. At that point, Wisconsin Natural Gas conducted an investigation and determined that all of the charges that were made to build up the excess balance were fraudulently made on the Providian MasterCard of John Kanauz. The $900 was not sent. Wisconsin Natural Gas ended up being out $4224.97 that the credit card company refused to pay due to fraud. Mr. Roussell provided detectives with a compact disk containing a tape recording of a phone call in which Linda Stephens requests the refund check. Detectives immediately recognized the voice of Linda Stephens as the individual seeking the refund checks.

Said reports further indicate that during the execution of the search warrants at the Stephens residence the computer belonging to Linda Stephens was seized. A subsequent forensic investigation of that computer revealed that the history contained numerous emails to Dell, Sears.com, JCPenny.com, Celebrity Curies and Northwest Airlines. The computer investigation confirmed that Linda Stephens had purchased airline tickets for a flight leaving August 22, 2002 on line through Northwest Airlines. The tickets were in the name of Linda Stephens, however, they were paid for with the Providian MasterCard of John Kanauz. The tickets cost $790 and were purchased in February of 2002 and mailed to the post office box of John Kanauz. All of the various emails relating to all of these purchases that were found on the computer were addressed to John Kanauz. The computer investigation also revealed that there were at least 35 payments on the credit card made between December 11, 2001 and February 11, 2002, and they all resulted in charge reversals due to some problem with the funding source for the payment. Various emails from Providian Financial reflected that the account balance was exceeded, but then subsequently a payment was received, so further charges would be authorized, and then eventually the payment would be reversed, so the account would again be over its limit, and the same process would be repeated over and over at least 35 times in a 60 day period.

Said reports further indicate that during the execution of the search warrant in March, investigators found documents reflecting that there was a fraud investigation relating to purchase over the internet, which used the JC Penney credit card account of John Kanauz. There were five purchases that took place after the death of John Kanauz. On December 10, 2001, the day after the death of John Kanauz, there was a purchase of eight $100 gift cards, however, that purchase was cancelled. Also, on December 10, 2001, there was a purchase of a Bulova Escapade Clock for a total purchase price of $60.12. On December 13, 2001, there was a purchase of a Holiday Angel Barbie Doll and a pair of Levi jeans for a total of $99.82. Also, on December 13, 2001, there was a purchase of a Panasonic VHS-C Palmcorder for a total purchase price of $642.15. Finally, on December 17, 2001, a pair of Docker's pants was purchased in the amount of $43.35. In the course of the March search warrant execution, officers found a pawn slip in the amount of $75, reflecting that on October 30, 2003, Thomas Stephens pawned the Panasonic Palmcorder matching the one purchased through the JC Penny on line account in Las Vegas. During the course of the June Search warrant execution, the clock and Barbie doll were both located inside the Stephens residence on Burdick Court. In the documents found, they also found a letter dated February 4, 2002 in which representative of JC Penney reflected their understanding that Linda Stephens, pursuant to a previous phone conversation, would be paying back $534.39 for charges made on the account of John Kanauz. No payments were ever made. There are also documents reflecting that John Kanauz had filed an affidavit of forgery prior to this death relating to his JC Penney account being used three times in May of 2001. The documents also reflected that John Kanauz had determined that his daughter, Linda Stephens, had used his account without his authorization. After he made that fraud report in November 2001, his credit card account number was changed to the *one that was used to make the purchases in December 2001, after John Kanauz passed away.*

Based on the foregoing, the complainant believes this complaint to be true and correct.

Ryan Park

This person I am supposed to call mother robs her own father on the eve of his death. In fact, she tried stealing from Grandpa Kanauz several times while he was still alive and he caught her and reported her to his credit company and had new cards issued. He knew fully that she was a thief and a liar and did whatever he could to protect himself against her. After his death though, she knowingly and maliciously took his credit cards and goes on cruises and flaunts financial windfalls by purchasing Picasso paintings. In my opinion, this woman has no conscience whatsoever. She cares neither about what she does nor whose she mows down in her path. In addition she lied to her brothers about their father's assets and kept them from receiving what was rightfully theirs. To this day, when these actions are brought up in court, she shakes her head no and says she never did this. It is for this reason that I use the investigative reports from the detectives. It is no longer my word against hers. It is proven evidence in a criminal case of deceit and thievery against every person she has ever known.

August 9, 2004 – The child abuse charges – What you are about to read here is chilling and I must say, these are just a few of the thousands of incidents we lived through year after year after year. As I said, I do not want to ask my brothers and sisters at this time about their experiences. They will tell their full stories when they are ready. Thus, below is the official complaint filed in Waukesha County on the 9th of August 2004:

Detective Ryan Park, City of New Berlin Police Department, being first duly sworn on oath, upon information and belief, says that:

Count #1 – *On or about February 15, 2004 Thomas Stephens did intentionally cause bodily harm to a child to wit: Charlie Stephens contrary to Wisconsin State statutes.*

Dad saw some definite charges this time around. Mom's intimidation was delegated to and executed by dad, although I cannot comment on them without knowing more about why this happened over the years. I was personally shocked to see dad get charged with so much and that mom wasn't charged with so much more.

And further advising the court that the above alleged offense is defined as a Class H felony; upon conviction of the above alleged offense, the above named defendant is subject to a fine of not more than $10,000 or imprisonment of not more than 6 years, or both.

The disparity in amount of years for the various events that occurred is still mind boggling. Thievery, fraud and financial crimes receive more years of punishment than child abuse charges. This is something I hope I can influence as the years go by.

Count #2 – *Same as above except on or about March 16, 2004 harm caused to Charlie Stephens*

Count #3 – *Same as above except on or about March 20, 2004 harm caused to Nick Stephens*

Count #4 – *Same as above except on or about March*

22, 2004 harm caused to Charlie Stephens

Count #5 – *Same as above except on or about March 23, 2004 harm caused to Jeffery Stephens*

Count #6 – *Same as above except on or about September 1, 2002 harm caused to Jeffery Stephens*

Count #7 – *Between May 1, 2001 and May 1, 2002 Thomas Stephens did intentionally cause bodily harm to a child to wit: Charlie Stephens contrary to Wisconsin State statutes.*

And further advising the court that the above alleged offense is defined as a Class D felony; upon conviction of the above alleged offense, the above named defendant is subject to a fine of not more than $10,000 or imprisonment of not more than 10 years, or both.

Count #8 - *On or about March 13, 2004 Thomas Stephens did intentionally cause bodily harm to a child to wit: Nick Stephens contrary to Wisconsin State statutes.*

And further advising the court that the above alleged offense is defined as a Class H felony; upon conviction of the above alleged offense, the above named defendant is subject to a fine of not more than $10,000 or imprisonment of not more than 6 years, or both.

Count #9 – *On or about February 15, 2004 the defendant Linda Stephens did being a person responsible for the welfare of a child to wit: Charlie Stephens, with knowledge that another person intended to cause, was causing, or had intentionally or recklessly caused bodily harm to the child, and being physically and emotionally capable of taking action which would prevent the bodily harm from occurring or being repeated, failed to take that action, which failure exposed the child to an unreasonable risk of bodily harm by another or facilitated the bodily harm caused by the other person, contrary to Wisconsin State Statutes.*

And further advising the court that the above alleged offense is defined as a Class H felony; upon conviction of the above alleged offense, the above named defendant is subject to a fine of not more than $10,000 or imprisonment of not more than 6 years, or both.

Count #10 – *Same as #9 except on or about March 16, 2004 committed against Charlie Stephens*

Count #11 – *Same as #9 except on or about March 20, 2004 committed against Nick Stephens*

Count #12 – *Same as #9 except on or about March 22, 2004 committed against Charlie Stephens*

Count #13 – *Same as #9 except on or about March 23, 2004 committed against Jeffery Stephens*

Count #14 – *Same as #9 except between September 1, 2002 and June 15, 2003, committed against Jeffery Stephens*

Count #15 - *Between May 1, 2001 and May 1, 2002, the defendant Linda Stephens did being a person responsible for the welfare of a child to wit: Charlie Stephens, with knowledge that another person intended to cause, was causing, or had intentionally or recklessly caused bodily harm to the child, and being physically and emotionally capable of taking action which would prevent the bodily harm from occurring or being repeated, failed to take that action, which failure exposed the child to an unreasonable risk of bodily harm by another or facilitated the bodily harm caused by the other person, contrary to Wisconsin State Statutes.*

And further advising the court that the above alleged offense is defined as a Class D felony; upon conviction of the above alleged *offense, the above named defendant is subject to a fine of not more than $10,000 or imprisonment of not more than 10 years, or both.*

Count #16 – *Same as #9 except on or about March 13, 2004 committed against Nick Stephens*

Count #17 – *Between September 1, 2001 and March 23, 2004 the defendant Linda Stephens did being a person responsible for the child's welfare, did through her actions, intentionally contribute to the neglect of said child, to wit: Jeffery Stephens, contrary to Wisconsin Statutes.*

And further advising the court that the above alleged offense is defined as a Class A Misdemeanor; upon conviction of the above alleged offense, the above named defendant is subject to a fine of not more than $10,000 or imprisonment of not more than 9 months, or both.

Count #18 – *Same as #17 except committed against Nick Stephens*

Count #19 – *Same as #17 except committed against Charlie Stephens*

Count #20 – *Same as #17 except committed against Amber Stephens*

Count #21 - *Between September 1, 2001 and March 23, 2004 the defendant Linda Stephens did being a person responsible for the child's welfare, did through her actions, intentionally contribute to the neglect of said child, to wit: Charlie Stephens, contrary to Wisconsin Statutes.*

And further advising the court that the above alleged offense is defined as a Class A Misdemeanor; upon conviction of the above alleged offense, the above named defendant is subject to a fine of not *more than $10,000 or imprisonment of not more than 9 months, or both.*

And prays that the defendants be dealt with according to law; that the basis for complainant's charge of such offense is: based upon your complainant's personal knowledge and investigation into the above allegation.

Said reports indicate that Linda Stephens is the parent of sixteen biological children. Twelve are currently adults, however, four of them are children who had lived in the residence on Burdick Court until 23 March 2004.

Said reports further indicate that, on March 23, 2004, Jeffery approached an administrator at his school, and requested information on how to become and emancipated minor. Jeffery said that thing had become so bad in his home for he and his siblings that he could not stay there until his 18th birthday, and he did not believe that his parents would voluntarily let him live with an older sibling who was willing to take him in. Statements were eventually taken from him and the other minor children, as well as Suzy, who was still living at the home with the parents until March 2004 (Suzy was 23 years old. She never had the strength to live on her own and always seemed to gravitate back to the place of abuse – this is discussed more in the chapter about Stockholm Syndrome). *The minor and adult children of Linda Stephens who were interviewed are all common ordinary citizen victims believed in this instance to be truthful. As to the physical abuse and failure to prevent physical abuse counts, the children reported that when Thomas Stephens physically abused the children, Linda Stephens was home and had directed him to beat the children.*

As to counts 1 and 9 – Suzy reported there was an incident that took place on or about February 15, 2004, at the family home on Burdick Court. She recalled the approximate date because her parents had just returned from a long vacation at about that time. She said her father was resting before the incident and Suzy was upstairs. Thomas Stephens came upstairs, went into my sister's room and demanded that she check her brother's blood sugar. He has Type I Insulin Dependent Diabetes, and his blood sugar levels must be carefully monitored and checked multiple times each day or he could suffer serious medical consequences. After Thomas Stephens demanded that she check his blood sugar, Thomas went and grabbed Charlie, and dragged him out of his bed holding him by the back of the head and neck and then dragged him down the stairs. When her brother tripped on the stairs, Thomas Stephens began to kick him in the stomach and ribs with the inside of his right foot. Suzy said that, as he was kicking her brother, he had braced himself against the wall with his left hand. Her brother cried out in pain and turned away, causing the kicks to being to hit him in the back. As he was kicking Charlie, Thomas stated "come on you little fucker. I'm sick of getting up every two hours for you." Her brother continued to cry after his father stopped kicking him. Suzy knew that her mother heard what was going on, because at one point her mother called upstairs yelling Tom's name. According to the minor children, Suzy and the records of the New Berlin police department and the Waukesha County Department of Human Services, Linda never made any report of this, or any other incident of physical abuse and did not take any steps to prevent subsequent abuse.

As to counts 2 and 10 – said reports further indicated that Suzy reported another incident that took place some time on or about March 16, 2004 in the evening at the residence. She heard Thomas Stephens come upstairs to the second floor and, from her bedroom, heard what she believed to be the sound of someone being punched in the back repeated for 30-35 seconds She left her room, and went into the bedroom where Thomas Stephens and Charlie were located. She saw him punch her brother in the back one last time. Her brother was crying out and Thomas Stephens said, "god damn fucker, you don't know what you just put me and your mom through." Charlie continued crying and appeared to be in pain.

Thomas Stephens then yelled down the stairs to Linda that he had found the missing bus money. Linda responded by calling out "where is the bus money" and Thomas responded "god damn Charlie. fucking has it" Linda then told him to get it and Thomas then told Charlie "hey you little fucker, come down and give your mom the fucking bus money." Suzy followed as her brother went downstairs. She saw her brother and Thomas Stephens and his right arm extended toward her brother with his index finger pushed into her brother's cheek. Thomas Stephens' face was red, and he was hunched down to eye level, nose to nose with her brother and said "hey, you little fucker, if it was up to me I would fucking kill you. You're lucky for your mother."

Said reports further indicate that Suzy reported this incident had stemmed from a problem earlier in the day. Thomas Stephens had to pick up Amber and Charlie from school, because they allegedly lost the bus money that had been given to them. As this incident in the home unfolded Charlie located the bus money.

Said reports further indicate that Jeffery also talked about witnessing this incident. He stated that when Amber and Charlie did not return home from school. Linda Stephens told Thomas Stephens to go out and look for the children. Jeffery said he was upstairs when his sister and brother arrived home. He could hear Charlie crying downstairs. His brother came upstairs to the bedroom and told his other brother that "dad hit me."

As to counts 3 and 11 – said reports further indicate that Suzy described another incident that took place on or about March 20, 2004, during the day time hours at the residence. Suzy said she thought it was approximately 11:30 a.m. She had worked a late shift and was sleeping in her bedroom. She was awakened by the sound of Nick crying out. She heard her other brother and sister cry out "dad stop!". Suzy opened her door and saw her father standing over Nick's bed. She saw Thomas Stephens wind his arm back and punch my brother in the back with a closed fist. Thomas Stephens then walked out of the bedroom, stating, "god damn assholes." Nick was crying and stating "I want to kill myself." Thomas Stephens went downstairs, but came back upstairs a short time later. Suzy was not in the room however, when she went to Nick's room, he held up a mayonnaise jar and a butter knife and told Suzy that Thomas Stephens had just thrown those items at him.

Said reports further indicated that Amber told police she saw her father throw the open mayonnaise jar at Nick and said she saw her father slap Nick in the face with an open hand, leaving a mark. Amber said that Thomas Stephens threw the mayonnaise jar at Nick's head.

Said reports further indicate that Nick also described this incident. He said that the children had eaten mayonnaise sandwiches for dinner. Nick was the last to use the mayonnaise jar and forgot to wipe off the outside of the jar to remove leftover mayonnaise. When Thomas Stephens discovered the mayonnaise on the outside of the jar, he became angry, and brought the jar upstairs and yelled at Nick. He threw the jar at him, hitting him in the knee and splattering mayonnaise on the bed.

As to counts 4 and 12 – said reports further indicate that Suzy provided information about an incident that took place on or about March 22, 2004. She said that this incident took place in the evening, around dinner time. This was a rare occasion on which the parent fed the children something other than mayonnaise, butter or jelly sandwiches. The children were being fed spaghetti in the kitchen, and both Thomas and Linda were present. Thomas became enraged when he saw Charlie poke Amber and Thomas said "hey you little fucker" and then punched Charlie in the back with a closed fist. The impact of the punch caused Charlie's seat to rock back and forth, and Chris began to cry and said "I hate you dad." Thomas responded " you can join the long list of kids that hate me."

As to counts 5 and 13 — said reports further indicate that Jeffery reported an incident that happened in the early morning hours on or about March 23, 2004. Jeffery said that his father woke him up, called him a "piece of shit" and demanded to know what he was doing going to his brothers and sisters and talking about things at home. Thomas Stephens was referring to Michael who was an adult, apparently saying something to the parents about Jeffery complaining about how bad things had become at home. Thomas Stephens then hit Jeffery on the back twice with a spatula, which caused pain, and then grabbed him by the ear and led him downstairs to the kitchen area. Jeffery said that he was in pain and his ear was hot and burning. Thomas Stephens then went and laid down and told Jeffery to "tell mom what happened". Jeffery said he would not admit that he had talked to his siblings, but did tell his parents that he thought they were abusive and did not provide the right care to the children. Linda Stephens responded to my brother, "you're wrong, you're a loser".

Said reports further indicated that Amber also reported the incident in which she heard Jeffery get hit in the back with a metal spatula at approximately 2:00am on the day before children were removed from the residence.

Said reports further indicated that Charlie also reported that Jeffery told the other children that he had been hit with a spatula by their father, and showed Charlie the mark left on his back from the metal spatula. Nick also recalled the incident in which the children were asleep and Thomas Stephens came into the room to wake up Jeffery. Thomas Stephens hit Jeffery 2-3 times hard with a spatula, and then Thomas ordered Jeffery to "get downstairs, your mother wants to talk to you." A short time later Jeffery returned to the bedroom crying and said "I hate this family".

As to counts 6 and 14 said reports further indicate that Jeffery reported there was another specific incident he recalled that took place during the last school year while he was attending West Allis Hale High School. He said that one day after school at the home, Linda Stephens accused Jeffery of being involved in drugs. Then called him "little Ricky" in reference to his older brother who had some trouble with drug use. Jeffery denied the drug use, at which point Thomas became very angry and pulled him by the ear down the basement steps of the residence. In the basement, the father grabbed Jeffery, and threw him in the ground and then punched him in the back two times with a closed fist, causing pain. Thomas then told Jeffery to stay down in the basement to think about what he had done. This all occurred between approximately 4:00 and 6:00 p.m. and he was not allowed back upstairs until 4:00 am the next day. He was not given any dinner the previous night.

As to counts 7 and 15 said reports further indicate that Amber reported there was an incident when Charlie was younger. Thomas Stephens hit his head into the wall near what the children referred to as the square step on the staircase between the first and the second floor of the house.

Said reports further indicate that Nick also described this incident. He recalled it happening approximately 2-3 years ago. Nick said that they had been wrestling upstairs. During the wrestling one brother punched another in the face, causing a tooth that had been previously fractured and repaired to come lose. When Thomas Stephens heard Jeffery crying and came upstairs to see what happened, he learned that the tooth had been knocked out. Thomas Stephens then took Charlie to the square step on the staircase, had him sit down on the step and then grabbed Charlie's head and began slamming it into one of the steps leading upstairs. Nick said he saw this as he stood at the opposite end of the upstairs hallway.

Said reports further indicate that Charlie also described this incident. He reported that there was one occasion when his dad pounded his head into the staircase. He said that the incident involved him and his brother playing and slapping his brother and knocking out a tooth that had been previously chipped. He said that Thomas Stephens got really mad, and slammed his head and also punched him.

As to counts 8 and 16 – said reports further indicate that Nick reported and incident that took place at the residence on or about March 13, 2004. He said that the minor children were all upstairs watching television in one of the bedrooms. Charlie went downstairs to check his blood sugar. While downstairs, he snuck 10 mayonnaise sandwiches back upstairs. A short time later, Thomas Stephens yelled from the bottom of the stairs "where is the bread?" The children yelled back down that Charlie had brought it upstairs for everyone. Thomas Stephens then called him downstairs, at which time he said that Nick had told him to make the sandwiches. Thomas Stephens then went upstairs and slapped Nick across the face with an open right hand, which caused pain an left a mark on his left cheek. Thomas Stephens then told Nick to sit on the square step between the first and second floor.

As to counts 17, 18, 19, and 20 – said reports indicate that the four minor children and Suzy reported a wide variety of problems within the household, including the parents failing to provide appropriate food, the parents at times depriving the children of food, the parents failing to provide the children with appropriate hygiene supplies and opportunities for bathing, the children living in the basement of their residence and being subjected to the elements and vermin infestation, the children being deprived of natural or electric lighting sources in their rooms, the children being deprived of appropriate medical and dental care, the children not being provided with appropriate and adequate clothing and the children needing to resort to theft to obtain necessary food, clothing and hygiene products.

Said reports indicate that Jeffery reported he and Nick lived in the basement of the residence for three years, up until August 2003. During that time, there was a broken window in the basement, which allowed rain inside the residence and created flooding on occasion. He said that, in the winter the temperature would be below freezing at times. He also said that the family dog spent most of its time in the basement and was allowed to urinate and defecate in the basement which resulted in a horrible odor. He said that the moisture, stench and mold in the basement attracted mice, spiders, potato bugs and centipedes. He said that they were not allowed to go upstairs to use the bathroom because it would make noise that would bother their mother. Jeffery said that he and Nick placed their mattresses up on paint cans to help avoid the mattresses becoming damaged from the moisture. He said that the door from the basement to the upstairs would be locked at night, and they would have to pound on the door to get their mother's attention to get her to let them out to go to the bathroom. He said they would then have to go down the road to the Super America Gas station to use the bathroom. He said that frequently he and Nick would urinate down the drain, and on some occasions they also defecated down that same drain, because they would not be let out of the basement.

Said reports further indicate that, when officers from the New Berlin Police Department searched the Stephens' residence they did discover that there was a broken window in the basement, and a trail of mineral deposits that made it evident that water came in through that window on a regular, long term basis and was flowing through the basement toward the drain. They also discovered an overwhelming odor of urine and feces in the basement. At the top of the stairs, they noted an eye hook latch type locking mechanism had been installed on the outside of the door leading to the basement, apparently to prevent someone from coming up from downstairs. On the basement side of the basement door, they noted a number of scuff marks, scratches and dents that appeared to have been consistent with someone banging or kicking at the door to get the attention of someone upstairs.

Said reports further indicate that Nick confirmed that he and Jeffery had lived in the basement for a period of time and that they would be locked in the basement for long periods of time. He said the two of them attempted to break out of the basement through a window on one occasion, however, it resulted in the window being broken. The window was not repaired. Nick slept on a board that was placed atop paint cans, and said that he had been bitten by mice and bugs at night as he slept. He described a stream of water on the basement floor, and mold and "green stuff" growing off of the pipes along the ceiling of the basement. He also confirmed that the family dog was urinating and defecating in the basement. Both boys would have to use the sewer drain to go to the bathroom themselves. He said there were a couple of overhead lights, but no heat was provided in the basement. Both boys described a separate room in the basement that did have heat, electricity and lights, however, that room was off limits to the boys and was kept locked.

Jeffery reported that his parents never purchased clothing for him and he had resorted to going to the Goodwill store in West Allis to steal clothing. He said that Charlie and Amber had also gone to the Goodwill store to steal clothing on several occasions. Jeffery said that some of their older siblings gave them some clothing to wear, and had purchased them underwear. Jeffery said that he, his two brothers and sister were each given only one pair of underwear and one pair of socks and they wore the same pair all the time. He said they would only be cleaned approximately once per month.

Said reports further indicate that Nick confirmed these reports about the clothing. He said that Holly had washed some of the kids' clothing, but had actually thrown a number of items away because they were so filthy. An officer subsequently met with Holly, a common ordinary citizen believed in this instance to be truthful. She turned over some of the very filthy clothing that she had saved in zip lock bags. There was a bag containing underwear for Amber, a shirt for Charlie, socks for Charlie and socks and shirts for Nick. All of the clothing was in very worn and filthy conditional.

Escape from the Dungeon

Said reports further indicated that Amber reported she had one little drawer with her clothing, and she only had three shirts and two pair of pants. She said she had only one pair of socks, one pair of underwear and one pair of pajamas. She estimated that her dad did laundry about once per week. She said that her mother had thrown away some of her old clothing and had just recently purchased new clothing the day before police came.

Said reports further indicate that when New Berlin police searched the Stephens residence they discovered a number of receipts dated March 24, 2004 and March 25, 2004, after the children had been taken into protective custody. The receipts were for children's clothing items, and appeared to match up with the clothing items that the officer found during the search of the residence that appeared to be brand new.

Said reports further indicate that Nick reported he was proud to be the only one of the four minor children who had two pair of underwear. He said he had managed to get some money and purchased a second pair of underwear on his own.

Said reports further indicate that dental records were obtained for the four minor children. The records confirmed reports by the minor children that they had gone long periods with pain in their teeth, due to cavities that were not treated and they had gone long periods without being taken to see the dentist. The dental records reflected that, as to all four children, there had been a number of occasions over the years in which the children had been brought to the dentist, and the dentists had discovered decay that required some type of treatment. However, in spite of appointments being scheduled, the children were never brought in to have these problems addressed. Dr Limberatos, DDS a common ordinary citizen believed in this instance to be truthful, reported that all four minor Stephens children were examined in 2003, and decay was found on the teeth of all the children. Follow-up appointments were recommended on all of the children to restore the decayed teeth, however, the appointments were not followed up with, and the restorations were not completed.

Said reports further indicate that, after the children were taken into protective custody, they were all taken to the dentists, and all of them were in need of substantial restorative work as a result of long-term lack of proper dental care.

Said reports further indicate that, in addition to not being taken to the dentist, all four children reported they were not provided with toothbrushes or toothpaste with which to conduct their own dental hygiene care. West Allis Police Department records reflect that, in the summer of 2003, two of the minor Stephens children were apprehended for shoplifting at a Pick N Save store. The circumstances were unusual in that the children were stealing shampoo, toothpaste and other hygiene items.

Said reports further indicate that Jeffery reported the diet provided by the parents of the four minor children consisted largely of sandwiches that were either made with butter, mayonnaise or jelly. Jeffery said that the children did not get any meat. He said the parents did eat better meals that included milk, meat, potatoes and other items, however, the children were not allowed to have any of that food, except that sometimes the two littlest ones would get scraps after their mother was finished with her meal. The children would not get the scraps however, until they had sat out for some time.

Jeffery further reported that the only operable refrigerator was a counter top refrigerator that was kept on the kitchen table, however, this refrigerator was only for Linda Stephens' food and the children were not allowed to touch the items in this refrigerator. Jeffery, at the time he was interviewed by police, was 6'4" tall but weighed only 150 lbs. He also reported that food would be withheld all together from the children as a punishment, and the children would resort to stealing from the restaurant they would clean every morning with their father before school or from local stores. They would also get some food that would be provided to them in secret by their older siblings.

Said reports further indicate that, when police searched the Stephens' residence they discovered that there was a full-sized refrigerator however, they located a receipt dated March 24, 2004 with a hand written note that the refrigerator must be delivered by 9:45 am on March 25, 2004. It should be noted that, later in the morning on March 25, 2004, a pre-scheduled walk-through of the residence took place. Police also discovered food receipts dated March 24, 2004 after the children were taken into protective custody, for miscellaneous food and hygiene items indicating that the parents had made efforts to stock up the shelves to make it appear that food was available.

Said reports further indicate that Suzy confirmed that the parents usually provided the children with bread, mayonnaise and butter to make sandwiches, and no other food items. She said that the mayonnaise was watery because it was not kept in the refrigerator. She said that, on occasion, Thomas Stephens would bring up jelly or cheese and on rare occasions, peanut butter for the children. She said that the two littlest kids would sometimes get scraps from the mother, however, they would sit out for days before the children would get to eat those items. Suzy said that she would have to give her younger siblings money sometimes so they could get food. She said that, once per month, Linda would be in a "good mood" and would allow the children an adequate meal, such as spaghetti with sauce. The children would be given a brief period of time in which to eat that meal, sometimes as short as two minutes, and then would be sent back up to their room without being able to finish the dinner.

Said reports further indicate that Amber reported her favorite meal was a mayonnaise sandwich and that she ate very little else. She said that she and her siblings stole food to eat, and would sometimes spend their bus money on food and then walk home.

Said reports further indicate that Charlie reported the children were provide very little in the way of food, and that he had recently eaten a jelly sandwich that was hard and stale because he was so hungry.

Said reports further indicate that Nick also confirmed the reports that the children were given very little in the way of food. He said he would look through the garbage for scraps of food and would steal from stores to survive. He said that they had never been given any milk, and that there was no refrigerator to put the milk in anyway. Nick also reported that he occasionally ate from dumpsters and would sneak money to buy food, but, if his mom found out, she would throw away the food.

Said reports further indicate that, for the children who always had a bedroom upstairs, and even when Jeffery and Nick were allowed to have a bedroom upstairs, from August 2003 on, there were problems with the conditions in the upstairs bedrooms. All of the windows were nailed shut except the bathroom window because the children had taken the nails out of that window so they could sneak out to go to the Super America store to steal food. The children reported that the windows had been spray painted so that no one could see in or out and no light came in. When police searched the residence, they confirmed that the windows were nailed shut and painted over.

Amber reported that, when she got home, she would have to stay in her room all the time. The windows were black and there was only a single light that her mom controlled.

Said reports further indicate that Jeffery reported there was no lighting provided for the children upstairs. Amber reported that the only light upstairs was in the hallway, however, the children had to stay in their bedrooms.

Said reports further indicate that Suzy reported that after the children were taken into protective custody, her mother gave her $60 *to go to the store and buy sheets for the children's beds. Linda Stephens also gave Suzy several filthy pillows, and told her to keep them in the trunk of the car so that when police and social workers came, they would not find the filthy pillows. Suzy turned over these items to the police. Suzy also reported that, when the parents knew the police were coming, they contacted Suzy and told her to get cleaning on the house immediately. When the parents came home, they also were cleaning frantically, and Thomas Stephens was using vulgar language in reference to what was going to happen to Charlie. He was waving his fist in the air and said that Charlie and Amber were going to pay for what they told the New Berlin Police.*

Said reports further indicate that Amber reported she was only allowed to bathe in the home occasionally and, when she did so, she had to use Ajax for soap. Charlie told his doctor that his classmates made fun of him because of his body odor, which resulted from his not being allowed to bathe on a regular basis. Nick also told his doctor that he was made fun of at school because of his body odor, and said that he would try to take a shower once per week with Ajax instead of regular soap. Nick reported that he was never provided any personal hygiene items such as deodorant or toothpaste. Jeffery reported that he showered only once per month and his brother reported the same.

Said reports further indicate that Jeffery and Amber had both been prescribed Ritalin for Attention Deficit Disorder for years, however, neither child was ever allowed to take their Ritalin, except for the day before and the day of visits to the doctor. The parents would have the children take the Ritalin the day before and the day of doctor visits so that it would show up in a blood test. The children also said that the parents made the children lie to the doctor so that they would continue to get Ritalin. Jeffery was told to lie about his grades so that the doctor would think that the Ritalin was being effective. The children were told to lie and say that they were taking their Ritalin three times per day. They were told to lie to the doctor and say that the lower dosages were no longer being effective, so that they could get higher dosages in their prescription. When Jeffery met with his doctor, after being taken into protective custody, he did not even know what Ritalin was for. When the doctor explained what it was for he said that he did not think he was the type of person that needed Ritalin. The four minor children and Suzy reported that Linda Stephens was giving the Ritalin to Thomas Stephens so that he could stay up with her at night frequently so they could gamble at Pottawatomie.

As to count 21 – said reports indicate that police obtained medical records relating to Chris. The reports confirmed reports from the minor children and Suzy that he was diagnosed, at approximately eight years of age, with Type I Insulin Dependent Diabetes Mellitus, a serious and chronic metabolic disease. According to a report issued by Dr. Jordan Greenbaum the Medical Director of the Child Protection Center at the Children's Hospital of Wisconsin, in order for Charlie to preserve life he requires multiple injections of insulin daily and careful monitoring of his blood and urine glucose or sugar levels. It is also of critical importance that he maintains a predicable eating pattern and balanced diet. The content and timing of meals is extremely important.

Said reports further indicate that a statement was taken from Charlie's physician who has been attempting to treat his diabetes problem. Dr. Kim reported that he repeatedly explained to the defendants the importance of having him seen once per month for management of his diabetes, however, the parents, at the time the children were taken into protective custody, had not brought him in for at least three monthly appointments, and had brought in Charlie for only a total of nine appointments between 1999 and January 26, 2004. Dr. Kim reported that the parents consistently missed, or rescheduled appointments, and it was his opinion that Chris was not being properly monitored regarding his diet and insulin regimen. Dr. Kim noted that neither of the parents attended the education class that he recommended. Dr. Kim examined the charges and records from a monitoring device that was recovered by police and concluded that his blood sugar levels were routinely out of control. When Charlie was taken into protective custody, he weighed 79 pounds. In a matter of only a few short weeks he increased his weight to a more age and size appropriate 92 pounds. Dr. Kim examined Charlie after he was taken into protective custody, and determined he had sustained 10% damage to his hemoglobin, and body tissues and called this "total body damage" "unacceptable".

Said reports further indicated that Dr. Greenbaum also examined all the medical records and reports of the children relative to Charlie's diabetes management. Dr. Greenbaum concluded, to a reasonable degree of medical certainty, that the medical neglect of Charlie's diabetes put him at substantial risk of serious acute medical problems, including retinopathy and cataracts, eye complications that can lead to blindness, nephropathy or nerve problems, which can lead to kidney failure and the need for a transplant, atherosclerosis, which is associated with heart disease and stroke and other problems. Dr. Greenbaum concluded that the lack of care for Charlie's diabetes will result in significant long term complications that will likely have a tremendous impact on the quality and duration of his life.

Said reports further indicate that a statement was taken from Mary, one of the adult siblings, a common ordinary citizen believed in this instance to be truthful. Mary reported that Charlie was unable to effectively care for his diabetes on his own, and the parents were not providing appropriate supervision. She reported that when Charlie would have a high blood sugar count, Linda would give him a lot of insulin and then tell him to lie down. Mary said that, on one occasion when his blood sugar count was very low, at approximately 17, and Charlie was having seizures in the kitchen, Linda simply gave him a shot and a lot of sugar, but Charlie kept falling and tripping over everything. Mary said she was crying and telling her mother earlier that she needed to take him to the hospital, however, Linda refused to do so immediately. When she finally did agree to take him to the hospital, they found that his blood sugar count had elevated to an extremely high 1100. Linda Stephens lied to doctors and told them that the count was so high because he had consumed a whole two liter bottle of soda.

Said reports further indicate that Charlie reported, when he would be taken to the doctor for his diabetes, his father would lie and say that he had been feeling pretty good lately, when that was not true. The father would lie, and say that Charlie was active, even though he said he is mostly not very active and just sits at home and lies in bed. There would be occasions when his blood sugar would show high, and the father would lie, and say that Charlie had snuck food and would lead the doctor to actually think that was the problem. Charlie said that, when he would be at home, his blood sugar counts would go high and low, and he would feel nauseated, sick and shaky. Sometimes he would fall asleep and would not be able to wake up. He said, if his count was low, his parents would give him a whole bunch of sugar, which even Charlie knew was wrong. He reported that when he would go to see Dr. Kim, Dr. Kim would regularly request to see the diabetic counter, however, his parents would make up stories about why they did not bring it with them. He said they did not bring the counter with them to the appointments because the blood sugar counts stored in the counter were at inappropriate levels. Charlie said that he had never been on a special diet relative to his diabetes.

Based on the foregoing, the complainant believes this complaint to be true and correct

Ryan Park

Now.....there is not much to say after reading that report. The saddest fact of all is that it was all preventable. Everything set forth in these charges could have been avoided if mom had been held accountable 18 years ago. It saddens me that Charlie's entire life will be affected because of this. He wasn't given the care needed and it saddens me to see him fight to control this problem today. Another completely disturbing and awful fact is that nothing had changed since 1987. It pains me to know that these kids had to live in the same conditions that we older kids were forced to endure. About the only piece of solace I had was that at the very least, they knew they could call the police. Somebody had done it before them so they knew they had an option there. From what I understand, there were several attempts to bring the abuse to light but nothing was ever enough to bring mom in for arrest. Finally, all it took was one man, Ryan Park from the New Berlin police, to investigate one suspicion brought on by a guidance counselor at Jeffery's high school for mom's house of cards to come tumbling down around her. I can't bear to think what would have happened if this "one man" didn't care as much as he did. What would have happened if he didn't "ask questions" and follow up on the responses. I have so much respect for this fellow, who is five years my junior, for his level of commitment to doing the harder right versus the easier wrong. I hope there are more people like Ryan Park in this world -- it makes me want to stick to this endeavor and do my part in saving some kids who cannot save themselves.

September 2004 – Intimidation of a Witness – In this latest set of criminal charges, we as a family were well aware of mom's attempts to change the course of fate by praying on the vulnerabilities she herself instilled in her children. Mom did this in the 1987 charges and was completely successful. This time a criminal complaint was filed with Waukesha County in September of 2004 after she tried to get to my younger brother. Below is a copy of this:

Detective Ryan Park, City of New Berlin Police Department, being first duly sworn on oath, upon information and belief, says that:

Between August 2 and 3, 2004 at various locations including the family home, the apartment of a sibling in West Allis and other locations while traveling in a vehicle, the defendant, Linda Stephens did as a party to a crime contrary to Wisconsin State Statutes under circumstances in which the act was accompanied by an express or implied threat of force, violence, injury or damage, knowingly and maliciously prevent or dissuade or attempt to prevent or dissuade, another person who has been the victim of a crime, Jeffery from causing a complaint, indictment, or information to be sought and prosecuted and assisting in the prosecution thereof contrary to Wisconsin Statutes.

And further advising the court that the above alleged offense is defined as a Class G felony; upon conviction of the above alleged offense, the above named defendant is subject to a fine of not more than $25,000 or imprisonment of not more than 10 years or both.

And prays that the defendants be dealt with according to law; that the basis for complainant's charge of such offense is: based upon your complainant's personal knowledge and investigation into the above allegation.

Said reports indicate that in March 2004, the New Berlin Police Department took a complaint from Jeffery a common and ordinary citizen victim believed in this instance to be truthful. Jeffery reported a wide array of abuse and neglect that had taken place against him and his three minor siblings at the hands of his parents. The neglect and abuse took place at the family residence. As a result of the report made by Jeffery and other information obtained from his siblings, a 21 count criminal complaint was filed against Linda and Thomas Stephens on 6 August 2004.

Said reports further indicate that on 2 Sep 2004 Jeffery came to the New Berlin Police Department to report an additional problem.

Escape from the Dungeon

Jeffery reported that approximately a month prior to September 2, 2004, he was living with his older sister as a result of having been removed from the home of his parents due to orders issued by the Waukesha County Juvenile Court in a case alleging that Jeffery and his siblings were in need of protective services filed against Thomas and Linda Stephens. Jeffery stated that on or about 2 Aug 2004 he and his sister had an argument and he left her residence. He said he was upset and did not know where to go, so he eventually called his mother, who was still living in the family home. His mother agreed to come pick up at the parking lot of the Sentry grocery store in West Allis.

Said reports indicate that Jeffery reported that a short time later his mother arrived to pick him up. She was driving Thomas Stephens' work vehicle and Thomas Stephens was also in the vehicle. Jeffery reported that this mother told him, in the presence of his father, that he could call their attorney for safety and to recant the information that he had previously provided to the police. Linda Stephens told Jeffery that they would hire him a new Attorney and that he would go to jail if he did not recant the information he previously provided regarding the conditions within the home. Linda Stephens went on to say that while Jeffery would be in jail, the other inmates were going to "put their dicks in your ass." She also stated that he would be beaten up by the other inmates on a daily basis. She then directed Jeffery to contact his siblings, specifically his youngest two, and tell them to recant the information they had provided during the course of the investigation. Said reports further indicated that Jeffery reported that his mother initially wanted to take him to a hotel in the Wisconsin Dells area where is older sister, Lisa Stephens, was staying, however his mother wasn't able to locate exactly were Lisa was, so she took him to the Radisson Hotel where she rented a room for him to stay for the night. Jeffery stated that during the drive to the hotel, his father tried to speak several times, however, his mom would tell his dad to "shut up". Before going to the Radisson Hotel, Linda Stephens dropped Thomas Stephens off in the Orchard Hills subdivision, since Thomas Stephens was concerned about the consequences of having unsupervised contact with Jeffery. At the time this incident was taking place, the Juvenile Court had previously issued orders prohibiting Thomas or Linda Stephens from having unsupervised contact with Jeffery and his siblings.

Said reports further indicate that Jeffery reported that when his mother took him to the Radisson Hotel, she got a room on the third floor and came to the room with him. She stayed for about two hours and continued to talk to him about the need for him to recant his statements. She said that she would be getting back at everyone who had a role in the investigation. She said she would file lawsuits against his older siblings and she and her father would be rich when this was all over. She told Jeffery that if he does not recant, he would go down with everyone else. She also stated that she would be contacting Ted's contractor to attempt to compromise the trucking agreements that Ted, "Jeffery's oldest sibling" has with the company. She also said she would be contacting Jeffery's oldest sister, Jennifer (that's me)*, commander in the Army to attempt to compromise her position there. Linda Stephens told Jeffery that he should contact their attorney and tell him that none of the allegations are true, that while the refrigerator in the house was broken, the family went out to eat every day and that the children were not fed sandwiches for meals.*

Said reports further indicate that Jeffery reported that his mother left after two hours, and he was then picked up the next day by his mother, his father, and his older brother Ricky Stephens. This time, Thomas Stephens was driving. As they left the hotel, Linda Stephens again began talking with Jeffery about the need for him to recant and the consequences he would face if he did not recant his statements. Jeffery said that Thomas Stephens did not make any statements, but while he was driving, Thomas kept looking at Jeffery in the rear view mirror and would smile and nod his head as Linda was talking. Jeffery said that he felt pressured and intimidated by what his father was doing. Jeffery also stated that his brother Ricky and sister Lisa have been pressuring him on behalf of his parents on a daily basis to recant his statements.

Mom used Lisa and Ricky as her personal pawns through the investigation and right up to sentencing. Because she knew she would be busted for talking with Jeffery, mom would send messages and threats through Ricky and Lisa. They would try to pressure and coerce him into recanting his story or to get him to talk to the three youngest kids in their respective foster homes to get them to recant their stories as well. This technique unfortunately worked well for mom at times, but whenever I caught wind of this happening, I would try to run interference for the younger kids and alerted Detective Park and Brad Schimel. Because of our vigilance we were able to thwart her efforts about 85% of the time.

Said reports further indicate that Detective Park contacted the management at the Radisson Hotel and they were able to confirm that Linda Stephens rented a room at the Radisson Hotel on 2 Aug 2004 and that the room was, as Jeffery reported, on the third floor.

Based on the foregoing, the complainant believes this complaint to be true and correct.

Ryan Park

When I read this report, it did not surprise me in the slightest. The only way I can compare this situation is to an example of psychological warfare experienced in the military. If mom would use her powers for good this would be a safer country. She is so good at these tactics that she would baffle psychological operations units throughout the military. This type of coercion and mind control using innocent bystanders was mom's preferred method to disturb and disrupt the enemy, in this case, her own children, which is in itself a disturbing thought. These acts of intimidation are extremely dangerous because they are beyond control. Years ago mom faxed Ted's work and his commanders trying to get them to bend to her will. She would make up very detailed lies and stories to try and get Ted's bosses to fire him and cancel his contracts. She would try to contact anyone who was in charge of her very own children to try and get them fired because she thought those children were a threat to her. To this day, I have to inform each of my commanders about her in case she tries the same thing with me. She once wanted to control my life again and she sent fake red-cross messages to have the military tell her where I was. Red-cross messages are emergency communications which can be sent to any soldier in the world if there is a death in the family or a serious medical issue that the soldier needs to be aware of regardless of where they are in the world. Mom would use this as a way to find out my location so she could call my commanders to get me discharged from the military. The one thing she didn't count on is that my reputation is stronger than her threats and lying. What she didn't count on is that I played the role of counter intelligence and told all of my commanders ahead of time of her intent to get me kicked out of the military so when they received these messages, they would dispose of them. I even had a lawyer prepare a restraining order in case she continued with the process. What she didn't count on is my intelligence and resolve to resist her. She always wanted to maintain control of us every minute of every day, regardless of where we were in the world.

2004 – Suzy's charges - Below is the official complaint filed in Waukesha County on 5 October 2004 and the quintessential example of how my mother duped so many of us and used us mercilessly for her own benefit. She didn't care who she mowed down as long as she reaped the rewards:

Detective Ryan Park, City of New Berlin Police Department, being first duly sworn on oath, upon information and belief, says that:

Between approximately September 1, 1998 and November 10, 1998 in the city of New Berlin and other locations in Waukesha and Milwaukee Counties, the defendant, Linda Stephens did intentionally take and carry away movable property of another said property having a value great than $2500, without the consent of said owner and with intent to deprive the owner permanently of possession of such property.

And further advising the court that the above alleged offense is defined as a Class C felony; upon conviction of the above alleged offense the above named defendant is subject to a fine of not more than $10,000 or imprisonment of not more than 10 years or both.

And prays that the defendant be dealt with according to law; that the basis for complainant's charge of such offence is: based upon your complainant's own investigation and personal knowledge into the above allegation.

Said reports indicate that a statement was taken from Suzy, a common ordinary citizen victim believed in this instance to be truthful. Suzy is the daughter of Thomas and Linda Stephens. Suzy reported that her mother had committed check fraud on her Associated Bank checking account during the summer and fall of 1998. Suzy had obtained a copy of her credit report in which it is reported she owes a balance of $8,207 to Associated Bank, as a result of fraudulent activity on her checking account.

Said reports further indicate that Suzy reported that on August 28, 1998 Linda Stephens took Suzy to buy a car at Dodge City in the

City of Milwaukee. The salesman was John Doe, an individual with whom Linda Stephens was having a relationship with at the time. Suzy said she was told that she would need to open a checking account in order to purchase a car. Suzy was 18 years of age at the time and had never had a checking account. Linda Stephens took Suzy to an Associated Bank where she opened up a checking account by depositing $100 in cash. She was told that her checkbook, check card and personal identification number would be mailed to her home which at the time was the residence of her parents in New Berlin.

Said reports further indicate that Suzy reported that when the checks, check card and personal identification number arrived in the mail, Linda Stephens opened the mail and then gave the items to Suzy. Linda Stephens retained a book of the checks and told Suzy that she was doing that "just in case". A few days after the checks had arrived, Linda Stephens told Suzy that she waned to put money into Suzy's checking account. Linda Stephens asked Suzy to sign Suzy's signature and date a number of the checks, but leave the rest of the checks blank. Suzy trusted her mother at the time, however, she subsequently learned that her account ended up overdrawn. She said that in October 1998, her mother kicked her out of the house, because she had blamed her mother for the negative account balance. Suzy was also missing her Associated Bank check card, and she blamed her mother for that, since on October 7, 1998, Linda Stephens told Suzy that Linda Stephens needed Suzy's bankcard so that she could make some automatic teller machine deposits into Suzy's account. Suzy believed that the money was going to be deposited as compensation for Suzy working cleaning Elsa's Restaurant for her parents so she gave her mother permission to use the card to make deposits. Since Linda Stephens had opened the original mail received from Associated Bank, Linda already knew Suzy's personal identification number for using the check/ATM card. Suzy did not give her mother permission to withdraw any money from the account.

Said reports further indicate that Suzy reported that in early November 1998, Linda Stephens told Suzy that Linda wanted to make Suzy's car payment for her, so Suzy signed and dated one of her checks at Linda Stephens direction, but left the rest of the check blank. She gave this partially completed check to Linda Stephens. Later, in the mid December, Suzy was at her parent's house and saw a piece of mail addressed to Suzy and opened it on the kitchen table. It was a notice from Associated Bank that reported that Suzy's checking account had been overdrawn by approximately $12,000. Suzy became upset and confronted her mother. Linda Stephens stated that it wasn't her (Linda's) fault, but that the "IRS was involved."

Said reports further indicate that the collection agency for Associated Bank is Monco Services. A detective subsequently made contact with a representative of Monco Services, a common ordinary citizen believed in this instance to be truthful, who checked through records and reported that Linda Stephens had contacted Monco Services to offer an explanation for why Suzy's account had been so badly overdrawn. Linda Stephens reported that Suzy had been engaged to be married at the time the Associated Bank account was opened. Linda Stephens stated that a number of personal checks had been issued to Suzy as wedding gifts, however, when the wedding was called off, the people writing the checks had cancelled payments and overdrafts occurred. Suzy Stephens reported that she was never engaged to be married and was not even aware that Linda Stephens had provided that false explanation to Monco services.

Said reports further indicate that in late May 2004, Jennifer Stephens, Suzy's older sister, mistakenly received some mail addressed to Suzy Stephens at their parent's address. The letter was a notice issued by Monco Services dated May 27, 2004. The notice reflected that the total due on the delinquent Associated Bank account of Suzy Stephens was $8,207. The notice stated, "This acknowledges your promise to pay $150 by June 2, 2004. Your file has been marked accordingly." Suzy Stephens said that she did not *enter into any agreement with Monco Services. The notice had been addressed to Suzy Stephens, c/o Thomas and Linda Stephens, at their address.*

Said reports further indicate that your complainant obtained a copy of the bank records for Suzy's account at Associated Bank and went through the bank records line by line and check by check with Suzy Stephens. The account was opened on August 28, 1998, and activity on the account was uneventful until early October 1998. Said reports further indicate that the bank records reflected the following transactions:

8 Oct 1998 – check #294 for $195 drawn on a closed account from Linda Stephens to Suzy's account with forged signature by Linda.

12 Oct 1998 – Check #295 for $295 drawn on a closed account from Linda Stephens to Suzy's account with forged signature by Linda.

13 Oct 1998- #296 for $395 drawn on a closed account from Linda Stephens to Suzy's account with forged signature by Linda.

13 Oct 1998 - #221 for $332.47 drawn on Suzy's account payable to Linda under false pretenses by Linda.

14 Oct 1998 - #260 for $279 drawn on Suzy's account payable to Wisconsin Ins Plan with forged signature by Linda.

14 Oct 1998 - #297 for $390 drawn on a closed account from Linda Stephens to Suzy's account with forged signature by Linda.

14 Oct 1998 - #101 for $220 drawn on Suzy's account payable to Linda under false pretenses by Linda.

Escape from the Dungeon

15 Oct 1998 - #298 for $395 drawn a closed account from Linda Stephens to Suzy's account with forged signature by Linda.

15 Oct 1998 - #258 for $190.55 drawn on Suzy's account payable to American Family with forged signature by Linda.

16 Oct 1998 - #530 for $595 drawn on a closed account from Linda Stephens to Suzy's account with forged signature by Linda.

18 Oct 1998 - #222 for $180 drawn on Suzy's account payable to Linda under false pretenses by Linda.

18 Oct 1998 - #225 for $332.47 drawn on Suzy's account payable to Linda under false pretenses by Linda.

18 Oct 1998 - #531 for $695 drawn on a closed account from Linda Stephens to Suzy's account with forged signature by Linda.

19 Oct 1998 - #532 for $895 drawn on a closed account from Linda Stephens to Suzy's account with forged signature by Linda.

19 Oct 1998 - #227 for $592 drawn on Suzy's account payable to Linda under false pretenses by Linda.

20 Oct 1998 - #535 for $995 drawn on a closed account from Linda Stephens to Suzy's account with forged signature by Linda.

22 Oct 1998 - #223 for $389.24 drawn on Suzy's account payable to Terry Schueller with forged signature by Linda. A detective spoke with Mr. Schueller, a common ordinary citizen believed in this instance to be truthful, who stated that he used to work with Thomas Stephens and had lent him approximately $2000 that Thomas eventually paid back. Mr. Schueller believed this check was one of those payments.

23 Oct 1998 - #226 for $770 drawn on Suzy's account payable to Ameritech with forged signature by Linda.

27 Oct 1998 – attempted deposits into a automated teller machine using checks drawn on an account with insufficient funds that had been closed in Dec 1998 with ranges from $700 to $2000 by Linda Stephens

28 Oct 1998 attempted deposits into an automated teller machine using checks drawn on an account with insufficient funds that had been closed in Dec 1998 with ranges from $700 to $2000 by Linda Stephens

30 Oct 1998 attempted deposits into an automated teller machine using checks drawn on an account with insufficient funds that had been closed in Dec 1998 with ranges from $700 to $2000 by Linda Stephens

3 Nov 1998 attempted deposits into an automated teller machine using checks drawn on an account with insufficient funds that had been closed in Dec 1998 with ranges from $700 to $2000 by Linda Stephens

6 Nov 1998 attempted deposits into an automated teller machine using checks drawn on an account with insufficient funds that had been closed in Dec 1998 with ranges from $700 to $2000 by Linda Stephens

9 Nov 1998 attempted deposits into an automated teller machine using checks drawn on an account with insufficient funds that had been closed in Dec 1998 with ranges from $700 to $2000 by Linda Stephens

10 Nov 1998 - #151 for $332.47 drawn on Suzy's account payable to Community Credit with forged signature by Linda.

Said reports further indicate that records were obtained for the Bank of America account of Linda Stephens, which records are believed to be reliable. The records reflected that the account existed from August 19,1997 through December 1, 1997, when the bank closed the account. There was a deficit balance of $5,360.86 on the overdrawn account. The deposits that were attempted at the ATM machine occurred at the Super America store at the corner of 124th and National Ave. totaled $15,580. All of those checks were written on the closed account of Linda Stephens through Bank of America. Suzy reported that although she had given her mother permission to use her ATM card, the permission was given under the premise that her mother would be depositing funds into her account as repayment for cleaning hours worked by Suzy. Suzy did not give her mother permission to withdraw any money by any means from her account and was not aware while it was happening that her mother was "check kiting" using Suzy's account. Based on the foregoing, the complainant believes this complaint to be true and correct.

Ryan Park

This report documents Mom's unbelievable audacity while duping her own children with incredible reckless regard. I am trying to stick to things that have been investigated and proven to ensure I show facts instead of my opinions, but this is merely one example of many times mom took advantage of her children in this manner. Mom has stolen the identity of all her children at one time or another. My 13 year old sister had the electricity bill in her name, mom stole everyone's financial future and put us all into financial ruin on paper before we turned 18 years old. To this day, we are all still recovering from the far-reaching types of "abuse" mom inflicted on us. Another example of how she robbed us of not only a decent childhood, but also a clean future.

May 20, 2005 – Bail jumping hearing – On this day mom was brought into court for violating the conditions of her bail thus "bail jumping" and providing us a way to get her back into jail as soon as possible. She had been up to her old tricks again trying to manipulate the children so they would recant their stories. In the bail agreement, one of the conditions was that she was not allowed to talk to any of the four youngest kids in any shape, fashion or form, however, we all knew she would try. It worked in 1988, but this time it is different. This time, I am here – and I am strong enough to fight her for the sake of the four youngest. I knew every little thing she would try, every little way she would attempt to get to the kids to get them to recant their stories. I told the investigators and the District Attorney every move she would make and every time she had the chance, she lived up to her reputation. I wanted to be the face that caught her every single time. I wanted to be there to protect those kids from their worst enemy… their own and my own mother. It is my place to do this now, because I wasn't able to do it then. There is no way I am going to let those kids down this time. I am stronger, wiser, and have a set of shoulders that could carry all of the blame from that evil woman. Just to be sure, the district attorney also filed intimidation of a witness charges against her to thwart her evil plan of intimidation. I refuse to see her get to these children, but she sure has tried. She sent gifts, pictures and even had the audacity to throw a birthday party for the youngest to try and influence her. She wrote a 16 page letter to Amber telling her she loved her, that everything is almost over and she will be coming home soon. What mom didn't count on, was my presence. These kids had no idea what she was trying to do. They have no idea that mom only wanted them as pawns to get off on the felony charges of abuse. Seventeen years ago, through manipulation and intimidation she was able to get nearly all of the children to recant, but this time she had to go through me and I am immune to her tricks. Although mom was not immediately thrown back in jail for violating the conditions of the bond, the judge admonished her and Ricky and Lisa who played the go-betweens for mom to the kids. They too are her pawns and they just don't see it. After the judge heard the allegations he again ordered no contact whatsoever so that the children can have their peace. Then he admonished mom publicly in court for her attempts to manipulate and intimidate. This is a part of the process she never had to face years ago and it is the moment at which I first started to feel like there just may be some justice for her actions.

2005 – While waiting for the sentencing – Today I am 35 years old and I am still facing a mountain of dental work needed to correct my mouth. My first trip to the dentist after running away from home, I had to have about 30 cavities filled, which was more than I have teeth. Many of my teeth had two or three separate gaping holes in them so big in fact that I used to hold my tongue up the holes to keep the air out to avoid the sharp stabbing pain. Over the last 17 years I have had to have many more cavities filed and a total of 25 crowns done due to the complete and utter deteriation of my teeth. When I was at my parents, there was no brushing of the teeth on a regular basis. We often had to use our fingers to get the bulk of stuff off our teeth. When we did have a toothbrush it was to be shared by many of the kids, and toothpaste, well that was a valued commodity in rare presence. In 1987 all of the children needed so much dental work it was unbelievable, thus when the kids were removed this past year, knowing what I knew from 17 years ago, I immediately started working health and dental issues. I figured if mom was going to get them back (which we didn't know), at the very least I was first going to get them medical and dental attention. Strangely enough, the dentist who saw the children also was one of mom's many victims. She had thousand of dollars in unpaid bills and this dentist had no way to recoup for his services, yet he donated his time and efforts and got all the kids treated and every cavity filled within about two months.

May 2005 – Looking forward to the July 27, 2005 Sentencing – I write this book as the story unfolds before me, thus I don't know how the story will end. At this point I am still looking to the future and hoping that everything goes off without a hitch. Mom knows how to use delay tactics, thus Judge Kieffer (before Judge Dreyfuss took over) set some strict deadlines on the parties. The DA had a deadline for filing additional charges by October 8, 2004 and the deadline for both sides to file any pretrial motions was October 29, 2004. A trial date was also scheduled. Judge Kieffer imposed these strict deadlines, because he remembered what happened 17 years ago. Judge Kieffer was in Juvenile Court back in 1987, and he is well familiar with the fact that the case fell apart when my parents managed to delay things. This time, Judge Kieffer took the position early on that he is not going to allow any unreasonable delays.

The DA and I believed that my mother was constantly trying to get around Judge Kieffer's intentions. My mother has learned from her past experience that the more she can delay proceedings, the more likely it will be that the willpower of the other side will wear down and charges will go away. This time around, her failure to pay their attorneys is yet another delay tactic in her game book.

The DA promised all of us that he is in this for the long haul and that he stands by his word. It was obvious from the beginning that my parents were going to delay things. He stated repeatedly that in spite of the difficulty, it is time for the light of truth to be shed on our parents' activities. What all of us endured is inexcusable and horrifying. He has stated that it is a tribute to the strength and courage of all of the kids that we are all doing as well as we are. To make it through this he stated that we are all going to have to stick together and support each other. My parents have quite apparently resolved to make this as difficult on us as they can but all we have to do is tell the truth.

The DA, Brad Schimel, has been so resilient and immune to her tactics. He will tell you how skeptical I was when this process began in March 2004. I can say unequivocally that I would trust him with my own life. He has unparalleled moral character and I can't do enough to show my gratitude for his role in this endeavor. What I can offer him though, is my vote if he ever needs it.

On May 16, 2005, the last day possible, mom and dad accepted a plea-bargain. The sentencing is set for July 27, 2005. This will be the day mom finally goes to prison for abusing her children. So much could happen between now and then, but everything is looking like she will serve time for her actions. I suppose this story is never truly going to end and this is merely the end of this chapter, but hopefully there will be nothing further to report between that woman and her children ever again.

Chapter 4

Charge Tally 1987 and 2004

1987 – Charge tally – Below is the tally for the charges in 1987 that my mother and father somehow unbelievably escaped:

13 felony counts of abuse; 5 misdemeanor neglect

Count #1 – Class E felony; $10,000 and 2 years
Count #2 – Class E felony; $10,000 and 2 years
Count #3 – Class E felony; $10,000 and 2 years
Count #4 – Class E felony; $10,000 and 2 years
Count #5 – Class E felony; $10,000 and 2 years
Count #6 – Class E felony; $10,000 and 2 years
Count #7 – Class E felony; $10,000 and 2 years
Count #8 – Class E felony; $10,000 and 2 years
Count #9 – Class E felony; $10,000 and 2 years
Count #10 – Class E felony; $10,000 and 2 years
Count #11– Class E felony; $10,000 and 2 years
Count #12– Class E felony; $10,000 and 2 years
Count #13– Class E felony; $10,000 and 2 years
Count #1 – Class A misdemeanor; $10,000 and 9 months
Count #2 – Class A misdemeanor; $10,000 and 9 months
Count #3 – Class A misdemeanor; $10,000 and 9 months
Count #4 – Class A misdemeanor; $10,000 and 9 months
Count #5 – Class A misdemeanor; $10,000 and 9 months

Total: $180,000 – 30 years

2004 – Charge tally – Here is what they are facing today as we go through the process:

24 counts of felony and misdemeanor child abuse and fraud

1- Class H felony - $10,000 and 6 years
2 – Class H felony - $10,000 and 6 years
3 - Class H felony - $10,000 and 6 years
4 - Class H felony - $10,000 and 6 years
5 - Class H felony - $10,000 and 6 years
6 - Class H felony - $10,000 and 6 years
7 - Class D felony - $10,000 and 10 years
8 - Class H felony - $10,000 and 6 years
9 - Class H felony - $10,000 and 6 years
10 - Class H felony - $10,000 and 6 years
11 - Class H felony - $10,000 and 6 years
12 - Class H felony - $10,000 and 6 years
13 - Class H felony - $10,000 and 6 years
14 - Class H felony - $10,000 and 6 years
15 - Class D felony - $10,000 and 10 years
16 - Class H felony - $10,000 and 6 years
17 - Class A misdemeanor - $10,000 and 9 months
18 - Class A misdemeanor - $10,000 and 9 months
19 - Class A misdemeanor - $10,000 and 9 months
20 - Class A misdemeanor - $10,000 and 9 months
21 - Class G felony (intimidation) - $25,000 and 10 years
Class C felony (Suzy) – $10,000 and 10 years
Class C felony (Grandpa) - $10,000 and 15 years
Class A misdemeanor (Grandpa) - $10,000 and 9 years
Total in 2004 – fines up to $255,000 and 138 years of prison plus restitution to all of her victims named in these complaints totaling hundreds of thousands of dollars.

Chapter 5

Plea Bargain

In a letter dated October 6, 2004 from the Assistant District Attorney, Brad Schimel, we children were informed that mom and dad were offered a plea bargain as stated below.

The attorney representing mom and dad asked the District Attorney to put together an offer for quick resolution of the case. In light of the fact that he was holding out the potential for a very prompt resolution of all matters without any further difficulty to any of the victims and very little additional effort on the part of the Criminal Justice System, the District Attorney made offers that are considered to be very generous.

Dad was offered a probation recommendation, as opposed to prison. If my dad was willing to enter a plea of guilty or no contest to the count which alleges felony reckless endangerment of the safety of Charlie by not providing him with proper treatment for his diabetes and four counts of misdemeanor child neglect, the District Attorney would have dismissed and read-in for sentence the remaining nine counts in the criminal complaint. When something is dismissed and read-in, it means that the person cannot be sentenced on that crime, however, the judge can take that activity into account in setting the sentence on the matter for which the defendant is entering a plea other than guilty.

As to one of the four child neglect counts, the DA recommended that my father be given a sentence of time served, meaning the time he has already spent in jail under work release would be considered the complete sentence for that offense. For the remaining three counts of child neglect, the DA would recommend that the court sentence my dad to three months jail for each count to run consecutive to each other. Thus, the DA would be recommending that he serve nine months in the county jail. He would be entitled to good time credit; therefore, he would only actually serve three-fourths of that time. He would be able to serve his jail sentence with work release privileges.

As to the felony count for recklessly endangering the safety of Charlie, the DA would recommend that the court impose, but stay, five years initial confinement in prison and five years extended supervision. He would then recommend that the judge place my father under five years probationary supervision. This means that if my father successfully completes probation, he would not serve a singe day in prison. Only if he violates the conditions and rules of probation would he face the possibility of going to prison.

As conditions of probation, the DA would recommend that my father be required to comply with all orders issued by the Juvenile Court, that he pay child support for the care of his children who are under 18 years of age, that he have no violent contact with any of this children, and that he have no unsupervised contact with any of his minor children. The person supervising the contact with any of his minor children must be an adult other than Linda, Ricky, or Lisa Stephens. Finally, the DA would seek a requirement that he pay restitution for the fraudulent credit card activity that he participated in with my mother.

My father rejected this offer initially in spite of the fact that the DA was willing to recommend that he potentially never serve a day in prison. Given the nature and long term duration of the neglect and abuse that he inflicted on his children, this offer was a gift. By rejecting this offer, he made a conscious decision that he would rather see his children put through the difficulty of testifying against him than take responsibility for any of his actions.

The DA gave a deadline of May 16, 2005 to accept or reject the plea bargain and at the very end of that day, my father took the plea thus avoiding a trial. The sentencing date is July 27, 2005.

As for my mother, the DA was not willing to make a probation recommendation, however, he did make an offer which can be considered a gift given the circumstances. The DA was seeking a plea of guilty or no contest to felony recklessly endangering the safety of Charlie by not providing him with proper treatment for his diabetes, four counts of misdemeanor child neglect, and one count of felony uttering a forged check.

As to sentencing, the DA agreed to recommend that on the uttering of a forged document count, the court sentence her to three years initial confinement in prison and three years extended supervision out of prison. The DA agreed to grant her credit for the time she has already served in custody toward that initial three years, therefore, she would have something less than three years before she would again be released.

As to the recklessly endangering safety count, the DA agreed to recommend that the court sentence my mother to five years initial confinement in prison and five years of extended supervision out of prison, but then stay that sentence and place her on five years probation. If she successfully completed the probation on that count, she would not serve any of that prison sentence.

As to the four counts of child neglect, the DA agreed to recommend that the court impose and stay jail sentences concurrent with the prison on the recklessly endangering safety count, and then place her on probation concurrent with the probation on the recklessly endangering safety count. As with the endangering safety count, if she successfully completed the terms of her probation, she would not serve a single day of the jail sentences for the child neglect counts.

As to my mother, the DA would agree to dismiss and read-in the over a dozen additional counts that have already been filed against her. As to her probation, the DA would recommend the same conditions as my father's probation, with a few modifications. First, she would be responsible for a larger amount of restitution than my father. Also, the District Attorney would seek a condition where she be prohibited from any contact with any of her children, except Ricky and Lisa. If any of the other kids wish to have contact with her, arrangements can be made to modify that recommendation. The DA would also seek condition that my mother be required to obtain and maintain full-time employment so that she can make her restitution and child support payments and that she would be prohibited from using or possessing a computer with internet access, from using or possessing a credit card or credit card numbers and from using or possessing a checking account or any checks.

My mother also rejected this offer. Based upon the horrific nature of the neglect and abuse she inflicted on her children for three decades, a recommendation that she serve three years in confinement was a gift from the DA. He made the offer in the hopes we all could put closure on these matters without any further trauma for any of her children. In rejecting the offer, she consciously decided that she would rather see all of us continue to be victimized by having to testify against our own parents in court.

The DA gave a deadline of May 16, 2005 to accept or reject the plea bargain and at the very end of that day, my mother took the plea bargain thus avoiding a trial. The sentencing date was scheduled for July 27, 2005. Half of me wanted this to go to trial so mom could be sentenced to all of those years in prison she was facing, but the other half truly just wanted it to be over. As to the charges for which there would be pleas and those that would be dismissed and read-in, the judge would have to accept the plea agreement. As to the sentences to be imposed, the judge would ultimately decide what the appropriate sentence would be. Even if the judge imposed more than the DA recommended, the offer to dismiss and read-in so many counts was still a substantial benefit to my parents. In addition to dismissing and reading in so many of the counts that were already charged, the DA also agreed that he would not issue any additional charges. There are dozens of other charges he could have issued. Do I think it was just? Yes and no, the fact that she is in federal prison is definitely in the "win column" but I personally wish she had to serve more time. The silver lining in this plea bargain is that none of the youngest children had to get up and testify against their mother and describe the events as they are described in this book. That in itself would be like reliving the trauma over and over again on the witness stand. It is for their sake that I am glad the court battle settled in a pleas bargain and did not go to trial.

Chapter 6

Stockholm Syndrome

2005 - Cycle of violence and adult survivors of child abuse - It is often said that children who are abused or neglected are more likely to become criminal offenders as adults. I am happy to report that of the 16 children not one of them has resorted to abuse. We suffer so much from the pain and anguish, but we do not abuse. We have our demons to deal with on a daily basis, but we have learned from our past and we refuse to repeat history with our own families. Instead, we have learned what not to do, which is an equally important lesson. We are loyal to our families and we will protect them from the demons we had to deal with growing up.

Survivors of child abuse use coping mechanisms to deal with the horror of the abuse. One such mechanism, protective denial, entails repressing some or all of the abuse. This may cause significant memory gaps that can last months or even years, much like the disassociating I discussed earlier where we become numb to distance ourselves from the psychological and physiological responses from our childhood. I personally have dealt with substance abuse, self-mutilation and eating disorders, all of which I have conquered except for the eating disorder. I struggle with it to this day. In order to recover, I, as an adult survivor, must adopt positive coping behaviors and forgive myself for allowing the abuse to happen over again after I left home. The healing process can begin when the children involved acknowledges the abuse. Two of the children, Ricky and Lisa, refuse to come to terms with these elements of the recovery process. They are stuck and I wish I could help them, but this is something they must come to terms with on their own.

1970 – 2005 - Battered spouse syndrome, battered child syndrome, the Stockholm Syndrome and why so many reverted back to mom –

Before describing these various syndromes I must first tell you how I personally feel about both of my parents. My mother is, in my eyes, quite evil but I have a great deal of pity for her because I think she is so mentally ill that she honestly doesn't think she has done anything wrong. I also can't help but feel hatred for this woman who terrorized 16 of her children in such horrific ways, causing lifelong, sometimes irreversible trauma. I cannot look her with an ounce of respect and feel physically ill in her presence. I can only hope that some day I find the strength to forgive her before I die. At this moment though, there is nothing but disrespect.

My father is a completely different story. I know in my head that he was an adult in the house and saw everything going on but in my heart there are no ill feelings towards dad. Quite the contrary, I love him. I cry every time I allow myself to think of all the time I have missed with him over the last 18 years. I cannot understand his loyalty to her but I respect his decision to stay with her. Dad was a type of role model for me. He taught me so much and I must say that it is because of him that I had the strength to leave, survive and make it on my own. I pray to God that when Dad passes away he can see in his soul my feelings for him and how much I wish we could have had a father/daughter relationship. To this day, I find myself trying to impress bosses with my work ethic as if I was trying to impress my own father. It is embarrassing, because I am 35 years old and yet every day I work for this goal. I can't stand my own disappointment when I don't do things in a spectacular way, which is why I strive so diligently to be great in every endeavor. I cannot stand to fail in anything, because I want so much for word to get back to my father that I have done great and wonderful things in my life. I think I just want him to be proud of me. I don't think this will be a feeling I can shake for the rest of my life, but at least I "know" I am like this and can manage my own expectations of myself using that knowledge. At least this way, I can accept an occasional failure and not expect perfection.

These syndromes are the only explanation I can offer why so many of us including my father and myself felt compelled to go back to mom in 1987. It took several severings of the ties before I finally succeeded in never talking with her again. It took several manipulations before I wised up and walked away for good. Below is some information and how I explain what happened to so many of us. After these enlightening excerpts I will show how it applies to my father, brothers and sisters.

Stockholm Syndrome and its Effects on Trauma Survivors

Stockholm Syndrome is a marvelous coping mechanism utilized subconsciously by many victims of humanly perpetrated traumas. These victims range from child victims of physical, mental and sexual abuse to battered spouses and partners to hostages of political terrorists. This unique mental/emotional tool is used by the victims to help them stay alive, stay sane, and sometimes avoid being physically harmed.

Once the trauma has ended, "Stockholming" can transform from a coping skill to a maladaptive behavior. When this happens, the former victim may seem unable to stop focusing on the perpetrator(s). Some survivors have great difficulty finding and expressing their suppressed anger, and may go to great lengths to deny or minimize what was done to them. Some are unable to go on with their lives.

When and How was Stockholm Syndrome given its name?

Stockholm, Sweden: In the mid 1970's, a lone gunman was trapped in a bank after a failed robbery attempt. He ordered four hostages, one man and three women, to go into the bank vault with him. For nearly a week, they were his captives. They had to relieve themselves in waste receptacles. He repeatedly terrorized them and convinced them that he would kill them if the police tried to break into the vault.

The police finally attempted to free the hostages. Instead of welcoming their rescuers, the four hostages bodily shielded the gunman from the police. Later, one of the women announced she had fallen in love with him and planned to marry him after the completion of his prison sentence.

Most of the world was surprised by the former captives' odd responses towards the man who had kept them hostage and repeatedly threatened to kill them. Their responses were dubbed "Stockholm Syndrome" by the mainstream media.

What is Stockholm Syndrome?

Stockholm Syndrome is a mental and emotional coping mechanism that seems to be inherent in the human psyche. It is a way of forgetting, or dissociating from, one's own pain and feelings of terror, anger, and helplessness by focusing on the face, voice, odor, mannerisms, etc. of the abuser or captor. Stockholm Syndrome is subconsciously used by many victims to deal with dangerous individuals by mimicking them unconsciously, thereby enlisting their protection and kindness. By expressing sympathy towards the aggressor, the victim can sometimes avoid harm or death at the aggressor's hands.

Stockholm Syndrome isn't new. It occurs all over the world each day and probably has, for as long as humankind has existed. It exists in many homes where battering and child abuse takes place; in prisoner-of-war and kidnapping situations; and in many other situations where humans are being victimized and terrorized by others who are often bigger, stronger, and more aggressive and violent.

How does Stockholm Syndrome develop?

One of the primary steps in developing Stockholm Syndrome is to dissociate from one's own pain and feelings of terror, helplessness and fear by subconsciously perceiving one's environment through the eyes and mind of the abuser. This mental process is part of a dynamic known as "identification with the aggressor." The captive or victim imagines seeing the current situation through the abuser's eyes and mind while learning how to please and appease the aggressor, to keep from being hurt or worse. This tactic doesn't work forever, but it sometimes can be used to manipulate the aggressor into taking a less dangerous stance -- for a while.

In battering situations in the home, in-between times of normalcy are crucial for the Stockholm Syndrome to develop. If a victim of domestic battering is continuously harmed and/or threatened with harm, the victim may develop a conscious hatred towards the abuser and may become angry enough to choose to leave, if possible. On the other hand, if the victim experiences times of normalcy and even pleasure with the abuser, the victim may become confused and will be more likely to stay in the harmful relationship.

This also can take place in other captor/captive, abuser/victim situations. Anyone who works with survivors of humanly perpetrated trauma learns quickly that there is no black and white attitude, for very long, in survivors towards their former abusers. Confusion is the norm. As with battering victims who become lulled into a sense of false safety because of the intermittent periods of normalcy, other victims -- including victims of sexual assault -- can also become confused.

After all, they know or will realize (if they have been with the perpetrator for any length of time) that the perpetrator is also human, is probably emotionally wounded, and therefore cannot be all bad. Sometimes perpetrators go out of their way to share personal information with their victims and emotionally (and even sexually) bond with them, encouraging the victims to pity them instead of feeling righteous anger towards them.

Having bonded emotionally with former abusers leaves the survivors with conflicting feelings (such as anger and pity) and can generate illogical concern for the perpetrators' needs, while the survivors neglect and ignore their own financial, physical, and emotional needs. Again, this is because the former victims are still Stockholming -- dissociating from their own painful feelings and memories by continuing to focus on their former abusers' activities and lives.

Bottom line: Stockholm Syndrome is a coping mechanism, a disassociative device that helps to keep a victim sane and safe -- if possible -- in a dangerous and overwhelming situation. It is a sane coping mechanism that works in an insane situation. But once the danger is over, the Syndrome becomes maladaptive, and the survivor must relearn how to not dissociate from his/her emotions and discomfort and to not focus on the former abuser/captor. Sometimes this is a very difficult adjustment for a trauma survivor to make.

What are some of the effects of Stockholm Syndrome?

Former hostages and other survivors of humanly perpetrated traumas sometimes act in unusual ways due to the influence of Stockholm Syndrome, even years after the traumas have ended. This is not at all uncommon.

Denial is one classic indicator of Stockholm Syndrome. By continuing to excessively focus on the needs and activities of the former captor/abuser, who may deliberately change his/her behaviors around others to feign innocence, the former victim may become confused and may wonder if the traumas even occurred.

Dissociating by focusing on the abuser/captor may be necessary while the victim is in danger. In part, this disassociative process helps to block out the victim's fear and sense of inescapable danger, so that he or she can respond calmly, in ways that do not upset the perpetrator(s). Sometimes after the trauma is over, the survivor will need time to begin to reconnect with suppressed emotions that were simply too unsafe to feel and express during the dangerous situation.

Minimizing is another common trait. A survivor may decide that what the perpetrator did wasn't really that bad. "I'm blowing it all out of proportion." Minimizing can be especially dangerous for a survivor, because by not facing the seriousness of the danger he or she was in while with the perpetrator, the survivor may feel more tempted to go back to the perpetrator or to not be totally forthcoming in court when testifying about what the perpetrator did. If the survivor protects the perpetrator by minimizing the abuse, the survivor may remain the victim.

If the survivor was abused or held captive for a long period of time, he/she may feel that being free and not being controlled by another person is too difficult to do. Having a human controller to decide what the survivor should do, think, believe, and say after his or her mind was shut down for so long can be preferable. By looking to others to control his/her mind and life, the survivor might not want to relearn how to take responsibility for his/her newer actions and decisions.

Unfortunately, some survivors will gravitate towards controlling individuals and groups (e.g.: religious cults and even controlling "recovery" groups) that will continue the pattern of enabling the survivors to not take responsibility for their actions and choices. Choosing to continue to be controlled by others only postpones the day when these survivors will need to learn how to make their own life choices and decisions, and take personal responsibility for the consequences of their actions. Only then will they truly experience personal freedom.

If the survivor was isolated from society while being abused or kept in captivity, the survivor may need time to catch up on changes that took place in the outside world during the period of isolation. Even if the survivor wasn't physically isolated from society, the survivor may have been so focused on the perpetrator that the survivor blocked out everything else for that period of time.

The survivor may need to develop new friendships and a new support network (if he/she ever had one). Some perpetrators work hard to disconnect their victims from neighbors, family, etc. to keep the victims from being able to get help and break the perpetrators' control. Some families grow tired of trying to help a loved one break free. Some studies claim that the majority of battered wives leave their abusers an average of five times, going back to the abusers again and again before they finally leave for good -- if they are still alive.

Most survivors of humanly perpetrated trauma were encouraged -- by the perpetrators -- to internalize guilt that belonged to the perpetrators. This is called "borrowed shame." Part of the healing process is to "give the shame (really, guilt) back" to the perpetrators. This activity can be done by writing unsent letters to perpetrators, by lucid dream work, Gestalt work, and in many other creative ways.

For many trauma survivors, one of the biggest roadblocks to building a new life is their overwhelming fear of the perpetrators. Some of this fear is legitimate -- some perpetrators are so fixated on controlling their victims that they will go after them again and again, ignoring court orders for protection. Some survivors may need to relocate before they can begin new lives. Some survivors

Escape from the Dungeon

are able to confront their former abusers -- again, this can be done through symbolism, unsent letters, and so on. The confrontation doesn't have to be literal. By visualizing themselves confronting their former abusers, some of these survivors begin to feel their pent-up rage for the first time. Rage is a powerful force, if used for good. It can empower and can be a propelling force that energizes the survivor as he/she works towards building a safer new life.

Some survivors find that they have taken on the criminal mentality of their former captors/abusers. They gradually found ways to justify their abusers' actions and belief systems. This especially happens with child victims. Some of these survivors will need therapy to mentally "deprogram" and reconnect with their consciences, some for the first time in their lives.

Many survivors find that after they have been free for a while, they feel tremendous amounts of rage that they simply were not safe to express while they were in danger. They will need help and support to find safe and healthy ways to express the rage. Unfortunately, some victims end up becoming victimizers. You know the old story: a man comes home from work after being chewed out by his boss. He yells at his wife, who takes her frustration out on their child, who kicks the dog.

A batterer, however, may do much more than yell. He or she may come home and be sadistic and controlling, and may physically assault or rape the partner or children. When the partner is assaulted, he/she will develop rage towards the abuser, but usually won't feel safe enough to fight back. The victimized partner may then emotionally, verbally, or physically abuse the children or pets. Many of these victims, once they become survivors, will need to learn how to express their anger in healthy, non-abusive ways.

Survivors may have unconscious "triggers." These "triggers" can be verbal, audible, and/or visual. Triggers can involve scent or touch. If an abuser wore a certain type of shaving lotion or perfume, the survivor might flashback when he or she smells that same scent on an innocent person. Calendar anniversaries can be difficult times for survivors -- sometimes, the birthdays or wedding anniversaries they shared with their abusers can be days that they need extra support to get through.

Many survivors of humanly perpetrated traumas are unable to bond with other humans because of the mental, emotional, and/or physical damage done to them by their former abusers. Some are afraid they will be betrayed and hurt, again. Risking connecting with people who are mentally healthy and caring can be a very powerful and healing experience.

Other survivors end up with just about no boundaries at all. Some of them can't seem to stop talking about things that are inappropriate in certain social settings. They may still be in "victim mode" since they were not allowed to keep personal boundaries in the presence of their abusers.

Some survivors who were sexually assaulted numerous times, especially as children, may have become addicted to sex and may do activities that are sexually inappropriate or even sexually abusive.

Unconscious or conscious reenactments of the original traumas are not uncommon. Each situation is unique and each survivor needs to be respected for what he/she has endured. However, survivors must be taught that regardless of their traumas, as members of society they are responsible for respecting the rights and boundaries of others. If they were never taught how to do so -- some were raised and isolated by multiple perpetrators -- they may need role models and mentors to teach them how to interact appropriately and set healthy personal boundaries.

Adult survivors who were abused by their parents may need to grieve giving up the mental image of the fantasy parents that is paired with memories of good experiences they had with them. Usually, only after these survivors are willing to look behind the good memories can they acknowledge and work through the betrayal trauma and other abuses perpetrated by their parents.

For whatever reasons, some of these adult survivors are unable to go through this part of the recovery process. Even after some of them remember having been abused by their parents, they may prefer to cling tightly to the good memories and re-repress the painful ones. Some of them recant, deny that they were ever harmed, and even go back to their abusers to perhaps be harmed again once the honeymoon period is over. Some of them are then encouraged by the true abusers to sue their therapists for "planting false memories" of the abuse in their minds.

Hopefully, the survivor will begin to realize that he/she was lied to, betrayed, and selfishly harmed by the perpetrator(s). Once that happens, the internalized "perpetrator(s)" will begin to morph and become one with -- by integrating with -- the rest of the survivor. (Literally, this means that the alter-states stored in different parts of the survivor's brain knit together and share information as the survivor's neuron paths connect and relay information back and forth, sometimes for the first time. This is a marvelous and exciting natural process.)

If this healing process continues, the survivor will gradually understand and accept that the "perpetrator alter-state" or "persecutor alter-state" was really a personality fragment that was unconsciously created to protect the survivor from overwhelming emotions and perhaps physical pain, during the original traumas.[1]

The "Small Kindness" Perception

In threatening and survival situations, we look for evidence of hope – a small sign that the situation may improve. When an abuser/controller shows the victim some small kindness, even though it is to the abusers benefit as well, the victim interprets that small kindness as a positive trait of the captor. In criminal/war hostage situations, letting the victim live is often enough. Small behaviors, such as allowing a bathroom visit or providing food/water, are enough to strengthen the Stockholm Syndrome in criminal hostage events.

In relationships with abusers, a birthday card, a gift (usually provided after a period of abuse), or a special treat are interpreted as not only positive, but evidence that the abuser is not "all bad" and may at some time correct his/her behavior. Abusers and controllers are often given positive credit for not abusing their partner, when the partner would have normally been subjected to verbal or physical abuse in a certain situation. An aggressive and jealous partner may normally become intimidating or

---

[1] http://www.kathleen-sullivan.com/Stockholm%20Syndrome.htm

abusive in certain social situations, as when an opposite-sex coworker waves in a crowd. After seeing the wave, the victim expects to be verbally battered and when it doesn't happen, that "small kindness" is interpreted as a positive sign.

Part of the Stokholm Syndrome is repressing the bad memories and looking to the good. Dad did so much to make things bearable and in my head I understand the elements of this syndrome, yet I still consciously choose to remember dad in those good times – thus making me a statistic. Mom however, never showed acts of kindness to her children thus we feel no endearment for her. Below are just a few of the stories which endeared dad to us:

George Webb diner and coffee shop – Dad would often take us to the George Webbs down the street from one of the buildings we cleaned or he would stop for treats at the gas stations or at Grebe's Bakery. When we were on the freeway going home, we knew if dad took that off-ramp on 35th Street by Marquette University that we were going to get something. We would smile a little smile in the back seat and ensure we moved around enough so Dad knew we were awake and to get us a treat. Sometimes when cleaning Elsa's Restaurant in downtown Milwaukee, dad would tell one of us to call George Webb's and order hamburgers with onions... maybe that is why I like onions so much today. Those hamburgers, they got us through some rough times. It was a special bond we had with dad. When we were alone with dad, we were just a family getting by. We worked hard for him. We knew he got very little sleep, we knew what mom forced him to do at times and we knew when he did just a little bit more to give us a silver lining in our dark clouds.

Making us laugh – Dad would often just act crazy to make us laugh. We would be cleaning at Elsa's and dad was in charge of the front part. He would be mopping with his walkman on and just be dancing or singing or something silly. We kids would watch him and snicker thinking how foolish he looked. One day as he did this he finished up and put his walkman on the table. On the way out he asked me to get it for him and I think I dropped it and the battery compartment flew open... there were no batteries in it. I looked at my dad and he started to laugh a little bit because he knew he was found out. I don't know how many times he did that, but I got the feeling it was more than once.

Fake beatings – One thing I recollect clearly is a whole bunch of fake beatings dad would give us. Mom would send dad up to beat us for one reason or another and we would put our body up against the wall tight enough so dad would clearly be missing us with the belt. He knew it and just kept beating the mattress and every once in a while we got a swat to make us scream so mom thought we were being beaten to a pulp. Other times, Dad would come up and just tell us to scream like we were being beaten.

Remorse – The most important reason I guess I favor dad over mom is his remorse. I remember one time when we were cleaning and he had me drive the car. When he got in the passenger seat, he found some chip crumbs or something and instead of hitting my face that time, he bit my hand. I remember looking at my dad in such disgust. He wasn't like that normally and I remember being more emotionally wounded than physically. In fact, it became a source of another argument at home. I lashed out often which is probably why I got beaten so much but I remember telling my mother "What kind of a father bites his daughter's hand because he is mad at her?" and my mother's response was "Shut up or I'll bite the other hand". I just couldn't look at my dad, until, later that night he came up to my room and apologized to me. It was short and sweet, but it was genuine and effective. I forgave him that instant. Just the fact that he knew he did something wrong and he took accountability for it and made amends. That was all I needed. I suppose that is why many of us don't care an ounce for mom. She has never once shown remorse or tried to make amends for her actions. In her sick and twisted mind, she did nothing wrong. I think I pity her more than I am angry at her, but until she shows genuine remorse and starts to make amends, we cannot begin to forgive her.

Isolation from Perspectives Other than those of the Captor

In abusive and controlling relationships, the victim has the sense they are always "walking on eggshells" – fearful of saying or doing anything that might prompt a violent/intimidating outburst. For their survival, they begin to see the world through the abuser's perspective. They begin to fix things that might prompt an outburst, act in ways they know makes the abuser happy, or avoid aspects of their own life that may prompt a problem. If we only have a dollar in our pocket, then most of our decisions become financial decisions. If our partner is an abuser or controller, then the majority of our decisions are based on our perception of the abuser's potential reaction. We become preoccupied with the needs, desires, and habits of the abuser/controller.

Taking the abuser's perspective as a survival technique can become so intense that the victim actually develops anger toward those trying to help them. The abuser is already angry and resentful toward anyone who would provide the victim support, typically using multiple methods and manipulations to isolate the victim from others. Any contact the victim has with supportive people in the community is met with accusations, threats, and/or violent outbursts. Victims then turn on their family – fearing family contact will cause additional violence and abuse in the home. At this point, victims curse their parents and friends, tell them not to call and stop interfering, and break off communication with others. Agreeing with the abuser/controller, supportive others are now viewed as "causing trouble" and must be avoided. Many victims threaten their family and friends with restraining orders if they continue to "interfere" or try to help the victim in their situation. On the surface it would appear that they have sided with the abuser/controller. In truth, they are trying to minimize contact situations that might make them a target of additional verbal abuse or intimidation. If a casual phone call from Mom prompts a two-hour temper outburst with threats and accusations – the victim quickly realizes it's safer if Mom stops calling. If simply telling Mom to stop calling doesn't work, for his or her own safety the victim may accuse Mom of attempting to ruin the relationship and demand that she stop calling.

In severe cases of Stockholm Syndrome in relationships, the victim may have difficulty leaving the abuser and may actually feel the abusive situation is their fault. In law enforcement situations, the victim may actually feel the arrest of their partner for physical abuse or battering is their fault. Some women will allow their children to be removed by child protective agencies rather than give up the relationship with their abuser. As they take the perspective of the abuser, the children are at fault – they complained about the situation, they brought the attention of authorities to the home, and they put the adult relationship at risk. Sadly, the children have now become a danger to the victim's safety. For those with Stockholm Syndrome, allowing the children to be removed from the home decreases their victim stress while providing an emotionally and physically safer environment for the children.

Perceived Inability to Escape

As a hostage in a bank robbery, threatened by criminals with guns, it's easy to understand the perceived inability to escape. In romantic relationships, the belief that one can't escape is also very common. Many abusive/controlling relationships feel like till-death-do-us-part relationships – locked together by mutual financial issues/assets, mutual intimate knowledge, or legal situations. Here are some common situations:

Controlling partners have increased the financial obligations/debt in the relationship to the point that neither partner can financially survive on their own. Controllers who sense their partner may be leaving will often purchase a new automobile, later claiming they can't pay alimony or child support due to their large car payments.

The legal ending of a relationship, especially a martial relationship, often creates significant problems. A Controller who has an income that is "under the table" or maintained through legally questionable situations runs the risk of those sources of income being investigated or made public by the divorce/separation. The Controller then becomes more agitated about the possible public exposure of their business arrangements than the loss of the relationship.

The Controller often uses extreme threats including threatening to take the children out of state, threatening to quit their job/business rather than pay alimony/support, threatening public exposure of the victim's personal issues, or assuring the victim they will never have a peaceful life due to nonstop harassment. In severe cases, the Controller may threaten an action that will undercut the victim's support such as "I'll see that you lose your job" or "I'll have your automobile burned".

Controllers often keep the victim locked into the relationship with severe guilt – threatening suicide if the victim leaves. The victim hears "I'll kill myself in front of the children", "I'll set myself on fire in the front yard", or "Our children won't have a father/mother if you leave me!"

In relationships with an abuser or controller, the victim has also experienced a loss of self-esteem, self-confidence, and psychological energy. The victim may feel "burned out" and too depressed to leave. Additionally, abusers and controllers often create a type of dependency by controlling the finances, placing automobiles/homes in their name, and eliminating any assets or resources the victim may use to leave. In clinical practice I've heard "I'd leave but I can't even get money out of the savings account! I don't know the PIN number."

In teens and young adults, victims may be attracted to a controlling individual when they feel inexperienced, insecure, and overwhelmed by a change in their life situation. When parents are going through a divorce, a teen may attach to a controlling individual, feeling the controller may stabilize their life. Freshmen in college may be attracted to controlling individuals who promise to help them survive living away from home on a college campus.

Escape from the Dungeon

In unhealthy relationships and definitely in Stockholm Syndrome there is a daily preoccupation with "trouble". Trouble is any individual, group, situation, comment, casual glance, or cold meal that may produce a temper tantrum or verbal abuse from the controller or abuser. To survive, "trouble" is to be avoided at all costs. The victim must control situations that produce trouble. That may include avoiding family, friends, co-workers, and anyone who may create "trouble" in the abusive relationship. The victim does not hate family and friends; they are only avoiding "trouble"! The victim also cleans the house, calms the children, scans the mail, avoids certain topics, and anticipates every issue of the controller or abuse in an effort to avoid "trouble". In this situation, children who are noisy become "trouble". Loved ones and friends are sources of "trouble" for the victim who is attempting to avoid verbal or physical aggression.

Stockholm Syndrome in relationships is not uncommon. Law enforcement professionals are painfully aware of the situation – making a domestic dispute one of the high-risk calls during the work hours. Called by neighbors during a spousal abuse incident, the abuser is passive upon arrival of the police, only to find the abused spouse upset and threatening the officers if their abusive partner is arrested for domestic violence. In truth, the victim knows the abuser/controller will retaliate against him/her if 1) they encourage an arrest, 2) they offer statements about the abuse/fight that are deemed disloyal by the abuser, 3) they don't bail them out of jail as quickly as possible, and 4) they don't personally apologize for the situation – as though it was their fault.

Stockholm Syndrome produces an unhealthy bond with the controller and abuser. It is the reason many victims continue to support an abuser after the relationship is over. It's also the reason they continue to see "the good side" of an abusive individual and appear sympathetic to someone who has mentally and sometimes physically abused them.[2]

In this enlightened age we live in, we hear too many stories of the battered spouse. There are men out there battered by their wives, instead of wives being battered by the husband and in this case, my father is a perfect example in my opinion. Physical abuse was the most common, but mental abuse was very prevalent and can be just as devastating. Signs of physical abuse fade with time, but the emotional scars never go away and much like the Stockholm syndrome I described above, dad would never admit this happened to him. In some cases, physical abuse might be better since it can be proved. There is physical evidence in bruising, cuts, lacerations. Mental abuse can't be seen by the naked eye; but you check with psychiatrists and you will find that the mental "scars" are there and many cases, they never go away. They help determine how a person will live their lives. Maybe that is why dad is the way he is: why he is loyal to her, is bitter and has an explosive temper… because of the way mom has treated him for 39 years.

---

[2] http://www.mental-health-Michaelers.com/articles2/article.php?artID=469

Chapter 7

Letters to the Judge
And
Victim Impact Statements

While doing my research of the public records for this case, I discovered that many of the people involved with the case now, were part of the case 18 years ago. Part of me is saddened and yet another knows that these people will take action now while they have another opportunity. In one of the hundreds of articles written about our family I came across one that quoted Judge Kieffer and felt compelled to write him a letter. Below is the letter to Judge Kieffer who still works in the Waukesha County Courthouse.

Honorable Judge Kieffer:

My name is Major Jennifer Stephens of which I think you shall find the name familiar throughout your dedicated years as a Judge in Waukesha County. I felt compelled to write to you as I was gathering all of the facts from court records and newspaper articles from the 1980's and today. Of course, you have been a part of these actions in both decades and I wanted to pass some information on to you personally.

Sometimes I think that I cannot begin to understand how my mother was able to get off on serious abuse charges in 1987. Then I remember that it is my mother, the master manipulator. I can only imagine the stories that she must have spun and the many people that she had fooled. It does not surprise me because I often describe her in the following fashion, if you met both of us on the street and talked to us both separately you would think my mother was an angel and I had lied about everything. Although it pained me years ago to see her go unpunished for her years of manipulation, intimidation and prison like environment, I must say that I am happy now that there is a price to be paid. I am grateful that my youngest brothers and sisters, of whom I had not met until they were removed from the home on 23 March 2004, have heard the stories of our survival and have chosen to emulate those actions.

As I was doing some comparisons in the stories from 1987 and from today I came across an article where you were quoted and a portion of it touched me and compelled me to write to you:

In a 1988 news paper article in the Milwaukee Journal by Darryl Enriquez he writes:

After approving a lengthy plan that gradually could return custody of 11 children to their New Berlin parents, Children's court Judge James Kieffer said Thursday that he feared that the abused youths might someday become abusive parents. In the Children's Court hearing Thursday, Kieffer said he was confused by how parents could treat their children as had been detailed in the petitions. He is a father of two. "I have an understanding of your background in that physical and emotional abuse may have been perpetrated on you, and you in turn perpetrated that on your children," Kieffer said. "I hope that when they become parents they will have learned from this experience. I hope they can lead productive lives." Kieffer said he viewed many hours of videotaped interviews of the children about what had happened in their home and found all of their stores consistent. "Shocked, dismayed and outraged, I was personally as a parent to learn what was going on in your household for years and years," he said.

I want to let you know that we children of Linda Stephens (less Ricky and Lisa who support Mother) will not be part of a spiral of pain and a link in the chain of abuse. We all have so many issues to be resolved of which some will never reach resolution. We will **never** recover from some of the things that happened and some of the memories that continue to linger in our mind, some of which have come back to our forethoughts as this process has developed over this past year and a half. My hope is that we set the example for strength and resilience, my hope is that we can show through our experience that abuse is not an excuse for abusing others. That abuse cannot be used as a crutch for failure rather a catapult to succeed in spite of circumstances.

I have been so lucky to find success in the military that I thank God every day that I joined for it has helped make me the person I am today. When I had my daughter and son I was scared of the very thing you remarked on in the quote above, that I too would abuse my children. But I wanted to let you know something that I hope you consider in any future cases that you face. You had ordered court ordered psychological testing for all the kids in 1987 and I was a rebellious 17 year old who thought I was not affected by my life in the slightest and didn't need counseling. But I remember something that occurred in one of those mandatory sessions that I felt I didn't need. I remember telling this counselor that I would never, never have children because I wouldn't want to hurt them like mother hurt us. He said something that sticks with me to this day and is the cornerstone of my parenting skills. "Because you are so aware of the abuse you are more likely not to do it." This one comment makes me a better parent. I don't hide my past. I tell the daycare, if you ever are concerned say something. I tell the schools of the past and tell them, if you see something, please say something. Sometimes we cannot see the forest through the trees and I want to set the example for others to follow. I will advocate against abuse and domestic violence for the rest of my life, sometimes in small ways and sometimes in grandiose. That is why I attend every court hearing, I want to be the face that my mother hates, so the four youngest aren't held accountable. I have a huge set of shoulders and will bear that pain for them as long as it takes. I would rather my mother take revenge on me rather than those children. I wanted to let you know, thus far, you won't encounter a cycle of abuse from the children of Linda Stephens. We have failed relationships, some of the siblings have less than stellar work and school records but some of us are highly successful in our professions. Ted owns his own trucking fleet, Elizabeth is one of the top real estate agents in Wisconsin, I have commanded in the military and was the officer of the year in 2002 and am working on my fourth degree, my sister Andie is going to be a doctor, Michael is going to be a pharmacist. These are good things and I truly hope this will be the story over the next couple of decades as our roots are here in Waukesha.

Thank you, Judge Kieffer, for being part of the process and stating your opinion openly to my mother. My only wish was that 17 years ago she would have paid the price and four extra kids would not have been subjected to the abuse. But, looking for that silver lining, she will never physically victimize her kids again, although I will forever worry of the physiological trauma she most assuredly will continue to inflict when she is out of prison. I just hope she directs it to me because I am immune to her now and she cannot hurt me and I will fight the fight for years to come I am sure.

Thank you again and know that we are survivors and achievers with the ultimate survival instinct.

With respect,
Major Jennifer Stephens

Jennifer's Victim Impact Statement – Below is a copy of the statement I made in court on July 27, 2005 and was a long time in the making. I had to capture all of my feelings and everything I had ever wanted to say in a ten minute stand to the court. This was an opportunity none of the children chose to pass up – it would be our only chance in our lifetime to address our parents, especially our mother, without her being able to respond back. It took all I had to stand up there in front of the judge with confidence and poise. When I spoke my first two words, "To dad" the tears were already in my eyes. This man was so important to me and now he was facing his retribution – it saddened me that he had to sit in those shoes and in all honesty, I wanted to protect him. That is what my heart wanted to do, but my mind knew different and I had to address him as the adult in our family. However, when I finished dad's part, my heart once again grew cold. I was able to refocus my purpose and talk directly to my mother without fear of retribution or violence and manipulation. It was the only time in 35 years that I have been able to confront her like that and I am grateful for the opportunity to put closure on how I feel about her and her reprehensible actions. I think my mother expected far worse than I gave. I was told that she thought I was going to be completely vengeful and spiteful in my remarks. What she doesn't know is who I am and what I stand for. She knows nothing about me. She doesn't know that these comments are made to protect those around me, not to avenge my own awful feelings towards her. I am the suedo matriarch of the family and it is my place to set the example for poise and grace under pressure. That was my intent when I spoke and I can only hope that it comes across that way when it is read.

Escape from the Dungeon

To Dad – I have lost what I have wanted the most in my life, a dad that I can tell all of my hopes and dreams to, a dad that I could cry to when my life was miserable beyond all recognition. My heart always has and always will ache for that type of unconditional love. Over the last 35 years I have heard that you hate me and never want to talk to me again. Over the years I have heard you stand by Linda with loyalty. I can never begin to understand the hold she has over you nor the love you have for her but I commend you for your loyalty to her. The day we talked in Juvenile court was the first meaningful conversation I had with you in two decades. It was the first time I hugged my father in two decades. It was a good conversation. It was a good moment – I choose to live with that moment forever because to me, whether it is true or not, it felt genuine. I will never know how you really feel and I will always question what is true. Instead, since I will probably never in my life talk to you again due to your allegiance to Linda today, I want to tell you something. During the time that I knew you growing up, you made the most unbearable days bearable. Whether it was taking us for a secret hamburger or sweet roll or when you would dance in the aisles of cleaning to your walkman that had no batteries. You showed me dedication to the end and you showed me unconditional loyalty even if it was to your wife versus your children. I sometimes see you as a victim, but also a responsible adult that could have changed history, but more of a victim of Linda. I wear my heart on my sleeve dad, what you see is what you get. I don't lie, cheat or steal and everything I do in my life is moral, ethical and legal because I feel at peace with myself living that way. Knowing that, I want you to know I love and care for you, I always have and I always will. I wish to God you could have seen my children as they grew up. I wish to God my kids could see the man I pictured in my head all of these years. Anything good that I gained from growing up at home was gained from you. The sales techniques, the ever positive outlook, the unconditional loyalty even if you can't understand it to those you have committed to. Much like you, I have committed myself too. But I have committed myself to my younger brothers and sisters and to my own children. If I ever had to choose between my children and a spouse, I would choose my children because it is my mission to be their champion and their savior and their mentor. I am not here to be popular, a friend, or a buddy, I am here to make sure the right things are being done. Most of this mess over the last year has not been directed to you, this has been pursued solely to protect four young kids and that is all. I hope you can see me for the person I am and not the person that mom describes me to be or sometimes the person you picture me to be. I will always do the right thing, no matter how difficult the circumstance or how difficult the road. I will always wish a better life for you. Grandma and Grandpa Stephens talked about you with such admiration every time I stayed with them in the years before they died. They talked about the man you were and all of the good things they remembered and the man they hoped you once again would be. Just recently I saw notes written by Grandpa Stephens on his death bed, they were deathbed wishes for you and your children. I wish you could have seen the things I have seen, Grandpa and Grandma always held out hope until they met their maker. Dad, they loved you to the end, believe me, I was there. Today, this is also an opportunity for me to convey this to you on their behalf. I hope it is something you can see as a genuine act of kindness.

To the Honorable Judge Dreyfuss who presides over this case today: The one thing that I implore on you that you most assuredly know, is that you have a distinct opportunity to assist in breaking the chain of abuse. You have the opportunity to give 14 of the 16 children a few years of relief from the years and years of manipulation and pain. I want to read something that Judge Kieffer, who presided over this case the first time these charges came to forwishen, stated in court on the very same sentencing day over 18 years ago.

After approving a lengthy plan that gradually could return custody of 11 children to their New Berlin parents, Children's court Judge James Kieffer said Thursday that he feared that the abused youths might someday become abusive parents. In the Children's Court hearing Thursday, Kieffer said he was confused by how parents could treat their children as had been detailed in the petitions. He is a father of two. "I have an understanding of your background in that physical and emotional abuse may have been perpetrated on you, and you in turn perpetrated that on your children," Kieffer said. "I hope that when they become parents they will have learned from this experience. I hope they can lead productive lives." Kieffer said he viewed many hours of videotaped interviews of the children about what had happened in their home and found all of their stores consistent. "Shocked, dismayed and outraged, I was personally as a parent to learn what was going on in your household for years and years," he said.

Judge Dreyfuss your honor, I must tell you that after that lengthy and painful endeavor years and years ago, many of us survived and thrived in spite of the circumstances that we lived in whether it was from living foster home to foster home, family to family and living the life of hard knocks. After hearing everything you have heard this past year, after hearing everything that you heard today, please sir, see that the past has come back to haunt us who didn't do enough years ago. These young children have an opportunity here, they have the opportunity to experience a normal life, to call friends, to have friends, to eat food when they are hungry, to use the bathroom when they have to, to just do the very minimum things that my mother could not, and worse yet, would not provide for them 16 times over. Judge if you decide to put my mother in prison for just a few years, she may very well come to realize the type of prison that she has put her children for decades upon decades. I will respect any decision that you make, but the decision will affect all of us for the rest of our lives.

To Linda Stephens – I stand before you today as the oldest daughter in the family of sixteen children. You may have given birth to me, but you do not know me. You do not know the pain that you have put me through in my own personal life, and you do not know the tears that I shed for my brothers and sisters knowing that it was needless. I call you Linda so much in my life because, in my opinion, you aren't a mother to me.

When I left your house and began my life on my own, only then did I begin to realize what had happened and the impact that it would have on me for the rest of my life. Much to your detriment, I am a very strong person, and I will never go away. I will be the most vocal person in defending the rights of those who do not have the ability or strength to do it on their own. I will shed light on this most unpleasant life that you yourself have created. If you don't like me, if you don't like the fact that I am standing in the forefront to be there for brothers and sisters that I have only met a year ago, just remember, you created me. But I, unlike yourself, choose to use that gift of strength and dedication granted to me by the grace of God for good rather than the manipulating evil that you exert on every person that you come in contact with. I would rather that you focus all of your hatred onto me, I would rather that you blame me for your life being so much less than stellar. Because, if you hate me and if you spend so much energy on trying to ruin me, then you aren't focusing on the youngest of the children. I will throw myself on the grenade for them every time, every single time. I only hope and pray that my strength and willingness to take the very long and difficult road of doing the harder right over the easier wrong sets an example for every one of my brothers and sisters. I love them, good bad and ugly, they are my family and I accept them as they are. No one is better than the other and we all will succeed in spite of the circumstances that you have dealt us.

When I had my daughter over 10 years ago, all I could do is cry, not out of joy but out of pity for you. How could a human being with any ounce of conscience beat their infant son in front of the rest of the children to confess for taking a cookie. How could a mother with an ounce of feeling for their oldest son tie him up naked in the basement with a humidifier cord and beat him in front of us to set an example of him. How could a mother with an ounce of dignity say repeatedly that she will ruin her children forever if they go against her. What kind of mother would forge prescriptions and force her 8 year old daughter to go to the Police and say she did it and then make her go to the doctor himself and admit to a crime that she didn't commit just so you wouldn't get caught. What type of mother would forge thousands upon thousands on their own children's bank accounts and ruin their credit history with such reckless regard for their well being? How conceited you are to say that you are so strong and powerful that you can affect the successes of your children. How conceited are you to think you have such control over us that we won't stand up and defend ourselves against you. These children have chosen to fight and succeed in life in spite of your influences. How can a mother want to take so much pride in trying to ruin the lives of her children both young and old. How can a mother financially ruin so many of her children for her own gain for frivolous things. You have destroyed the lives of so many of your children and the absolute worst part of it is that you don't care, you have not one ounce of remorse, and you unequivocally refuse to accept responsibility for your actions. You have gone far too long without being held accountable, and that is about to change. How could you as the Daughter of Grandpa Kanauz steal from him moments after he died and charge almost $50,000 dollars on his credit cards, book Celebrity Cruises, airline tickets and hotel rooms in San Juan and Las Vegas for your vacations. How could you steal his car and belongings from his apartment before you even identify his body in the morgue?

You manipulate and intimidate your children – you stole their identities, you ruined their credit for years to come, you stole their innocence without remorse, you took advantage of your father and stole tens of thousands of dollars after his death and put his ashes in a BBQ grill on your patio, you took advantage of your brothers, you took advantage of your mother and father in law, you took advantage of an innocent man from Florida that you had an illicit affair with and ruined his life and now he hangs his head in shame for knowing you, you use my father as your own personal pawn, my question for you.....is there anyone on this earth that you wouldn't hurt besides yourself? We will no longer be your pawns.

I am often asked what I think would be a fair punishment for the things that you have done and only one word comes to my mind, prison – In my opinion, you affected 16 children over 35 years and should have to serve 35 years in prison much like the one that you provided for us. I wonder how you would react if you were tied up and beaten like you did to your son, I wonder how you would act if you were shoved up on a wall and had your hair chopped off. I wonder how you would feel if you had defecated and urinated right next to your bed. I want to see you in prison when you are locked in your cell and it is 120 degrees with no lights and you are laying on the floor next to the bottom of the door trying to get a whiff of fresh air. I wonder if you would think you are being abused or if you would think it is normal and not abusive at all. I want to see someone steal hundreds of thousands of dollars and your identity. I want someone to steal your credit cards moments after you die and see what your reaction would be. This would be fair in my eyes – getting what you gave to us for 35 years.

Linda, I only hope that you will be given time to reflect on the damage that you have inflicted and that when you are released from your time in prison if you are so granted that time here today, that you move on with your life and leave your children alone who want to be left alone, so that they may prosper and raise children of their own in a normal fashion. I pray to God that the chain of abuse stops with the sixteen of us. I pray to God that we defy the law of averages and no one slips down the slippery slope of manipulation and thievery and threats that you call normal every day occurrences. I don't hate you, but I do pity you. I don't respect you as a mother, a wife, a friend or as a human being, and as of today, I still cannot find it in my heart to yet forgive you because I see that the same abuse you inflicted onto me has been inflicted on all 15 of my brothers and sisters. I thank god that I have the one thing you will never get from any of your 16 children, the respect and admiration of my son and daughter. I pray that God has Mercy on you and can show you the forgiveness that I cannot find in my heart to give you today or any day in the foreseeable future, and that is all that I have to say to you both today and for the rest of your life.

Holly's Victim Impact Statement – Holly wrote this to mom and dad on July 27, 2005:

I'd like to address this to my parents, which is ironic because in my eyes, I no longer have parents. First, I'd like to start with the definition of a parent: A parent is who brings up and cares for another. A mother is someone who gives birth and then both of the mother and the father should protect and teach the moral values in their life. That child should be able to depend on the parents in any type of situation that arises in their life. Parents are there to give advice to the child and teach the child right from wrong. It is a parent's responsibility to steer that child in the right direction from peer pressure, abstinence, drugs, alcohol, education, respecting your elders, responsibility, etc. A parent should be there to comfort that child when they get hurt or sick.

Mom, Dad you did none of the things that a parent should in my eyes. I, as a parent, try and do the best for my children and that is all they expect out of me. They know there is no such thing as a perfect parent but you made it possible for me to visualize the worst parents I will ever know. I need to ask this as I am sure all the kids here today are wondering the same thing: why in the hell did you have us? Why waste the time having kids when you couldn't handle nor afford it? We don't understand why have kids when you couldn't love, care, nurture, guide, respect, cuddle, protect, and to be true to the child. If you did show us any act of kindness it was for your own personal gain. All that you thought of mom was "what can Linda get out of it?" I don't understand this type of thinking.

Do you even know how a mother is supposed to act? I continue to wonder that. You never showed any type of affection to any of us. Remember you didn't even call us by our own names most of the time. It was always bitch, asshole, mother fucker, or even my personal favorite "hey Jennifer the 2nd." This is how I remember my childhood: closed, shut out from the real world, sheltered, scared, and meaningless, and scarred for life. I have so many bad memories from when I was a kid that I blocked it out of my head until about a 1 ½ year ago. It is only now in 2005 that I am learning how to deal with it all.

Remember the time that a cookie was gone and you had dad line us up in front of you in the family room? You had Jamie, who was 8 months old, in your arms with you holding the black strap. You were telling us to confess who took the cookie or Jeffrey was going to get it. At the time, no one confessed. You took down Jeffrey's diaper down and started to beat him with the belt and were yelling as you did this to him. You screamed with a psychotic rage as you beat your infant son, "Who did it, who did it and they better confess or I am going to keep hitting the baby." Still no one confessed but I then took Jeffrey from your arms and that's when you really got furious. You had that possessed look that every single one of us were scared of – the "bug eyes". You told dad to grab Jeffrey out of my arms and to take me upstairs and beat me. I cannot tell you how grateful I am to you for those memories.

Do you remember the time you beat Jennifer with the long metal spatula? You just kept hitting and hitting her as she screamed in terror. Its like you both thrived on afflicting pain on your children. Jennifer tried to protect herself so much from the spatula that after you were done she looked at her hands and her knuckles were bloody from your wrath of anger. You did that to her and that is only one of the times that I am mentioning right now.

Another memory I have is getting up at midnight, at age 9, to go be slaves and work for my parents business it is no wonder why I suffer from insomnia now. I worked all night for you guys and I even got my school records and I only showed up for 80 days out of all the school years when I was younger. It is no wonder had a terrible time with school and my grades.

How about the hot summers that we used to spend in our rooms where there was no air conditioning with the hot air in our rooms while mom had an air conditioner facing her as she slept all day everyday? In order to communicate with each other within our locked bedrooms, we would talk underneath the door and have everyday conversations; this is how most of communicating took place. How demeaning is that? We would always get yelled at for this because we made too much noise and mom would wake up mom during the day. We couldn't even walk in our room because our room was above the family room where mom called it her bedroom. If we did walk and mom heard a creek on the floor shed send dad up to beat us and ordered us not to get out bed again. How do you treat kids like this I don't understand? The best was laying there next to the bottom of the door because the cool air would come through the bottom crack. We spent many days by that bottom of the door.

Then mom you had dad put door locks on our doors. Like having hooks on the outside of the door wasn't good enough and your reasons for putting them there was because you found out that we were getting out of our rooms to sneak food or use the bathroom. So there we sat now with the door locks and hooks on the outside of our bedroom doors and we were now your prisoners. What else do you call it? Life in a 10X10 room was our world. We had many fantasy lives in our room.

Escape from the Dungeon

Then we got older and mom became selective on who would be her pawn to stay down stairs with her if she needed anything while dad was at work. I was one of her pawns. I used to stay at the bottom of your bed on the floor in the family room and wait till you needed anything. You slept all day and everyday was like that. While laying there on the floor I couldn't make a peep. So we learned to act like a statue when you were sleeping and you were just laying there. Then mom you would have your usual commands as you woke up. "Go check and see if the kids got out there rooms, take the dogs out, call your father with the list, (meaning dad going to the store and getting food what mom wanted to eat that night). Go get me a glass of milk and DON'T touch the top rim of the glass (as if we had a disease or something.)" This was all normal everyday living in our house hold.

How about the times you used to kick dad out of the house Mom every single week. You would kick him out for anything you could come up with, Dad treated you like a queen and yet he got punished for it. After a few hours of dad being kicked out it would always be the same thing over and over. He'd end up at the air conditioner in the family room and beg for your forgiveness for whatever he did, which were completely insignificant. After you argued through the window you would demand dad to leave or you would give him a divorce. Eventually he left and would call you on the phone. You would pick up the receiver and hang it up about 20 times before you would have me answer it to do your dirty work. Dad would ask "can I please talk to your mother?" I would ask you if you wanted to talk with dad but the response was always vulgar language and you made me repeat it back to him. Dad would start crying and trust me no daughter in the world should hear this type of crying from her father. He would cry how much he loved you and then finally you would let him back in the house.

You always waited until he made a complete ass of himself until you were satisfied before you let him back in the house. Then everything went back the way it was – which I could never understand. Thank you mom for that memory. Mom, you didn't just manipulate and control your own kids but you did it to your own husband. But dad I blame you for not putting a stop to all this insanity. You let it go on and on. I could go on and on but then I would have to write a book.

Currently I am blessed with so many things that I couldn't even count or believe I deserve. I have been blessed with my husband for the past 6 years and he treats me like a queen. He respects me, he loves me, he takes care of me, he protects me and he supports me in any decision I make. In my eyes I am getting paid back for all the misery that I endured with you. I would live through it all again if I knew I was going to meet my husband. He makes me feel like I can conquer anything that I set my mind too. My husband and 5 kids are all I need they complete me as a whole person. I love my family. Why didn't you love your children like that, or love each other like that at the very least?

As an adult this has been really hard for me. I've blocked most of my memories until about 1 ½ years ago. I have been on anti depressants for 10 months I have recently found out I have 8 ulcers. I will be on medication for the rest of my life due to the stress. I didn't think it would hit me this hard because I have learned to block the pain most of my life. I can't believe that you didn't learn anything from 1987 and you went back to your old ways and raised these last set of four brothers and sister today under the same abusive ways you bestowed to us older 12 kids. The pain and psychological problems you've done to these kids is indescribable. When March 23rd of 2004 came and I found out that the

Escape from the Dungeon

kids were taken out I have to say that I was pleased. I went down to the police station with Amy and we were there for our brothers and sister. They were so happy to see us because you had forbidden them to see any of their older brothers and sisters. They felt comforted that we were there to rescue them. They were scared what you were going to do if they went back home again and we assured them that over our dead bodies would they be going back home because we knew what life was under that roof. After being at the police station for hours that night I finally took all the kids back to my house until we figured out what was going to happen next.

My husband went to go get underwear and socks and pajamas for all the kids and they didn't even know what pajamas were. You don't deserve to be in these childrens' lives and it has been very hard this past year and a half to deal with the everyday problems that these kids were going through while remember our own past. They were acting on what you taught them over the years. They are just trying to cope with what reality is to them today and I know it has to be some of the hardest days in their lives. I am so proud of these kids because they showed me how strong they are and how they stand up what they believe in.

The insanity has to stop here. Judge Dreyfuss, I ask you to take in consideration what I have told you today and what everyone else has told you. Set the punishment that best suits for destroying 16 childhoods. As for Tom and Linda, you are no longer my parents and I don't want you to destroy any more lives than you already have done. I can't forget what happened but I do forgive you. We can't go on in life dwelling on the past any longer and this is my closure to this chapter to my life. So I say farewell and you will meet your maker when you pass on to the next life.
-Holly

Chapter 8

Sentencing

Escape from the Dungeon

July 27, 2005 – Judge Dreyfuss was incredible. He not only allowed every child to make their statements, but said that it was critical as to the character of Linda Stephens and her propensity to abuse again and to take advantage of her children. Each child got up and gave their statement; each child described how they are affected today because of what mom has put us through. Each child spun their tale of manipulation, abuse and control that mom exuded over them and how they are affected today. Mom sat their stone faced without caring, just staring ahead with her jaw clenched. I was the last one to make a statement and when I saw the first two words on my paper in front of me, I started to tear up before I started. Those two words were "To dad". As I read my statement dad sat their crying. As I told him how I felt about him and how Grandma and Grandpa Stephens felt about him in their final years of life, he choked back his emotion. That was the hardest part of my statement because I will always love my father. After the statements were finished the defense began their case. Ricky and Lisa spoke on behalf of my parents and to say that they came off looking ridiculous is an understatement. It was as if they decided at the last minute to make a statement and their words were not thought out. Ricky attacked the New Berlin Police Department and the District Attorney with disregard for the efforts they have displayed. He defended mom and called her "a good mother". The only thing I can say is that he has not come to terms with the way we grew up. He is clouded in his visions and overlooking the bad that has happened in our lives…but, he has the right to back mom and dad up and he was afforded that opportunity. After they spoke, mom's lawyer tried to defend and mitigate mom's actions. He stated that mom was diagnosed with bipolar disorder in the early 1990's, Lupus and a variety of other medical conditions. Her lawyer attacked me personally, stating I was out for my own revenge and benefit. It was so clear that he was simply regurgitating what mom had instructed him to say. It was clear that mom was trying to belittle us and our efforts from the defendant's chair. Mom's lawyer painted a picture of such a state of mental illness that she had no control over the way she acted in the last few years. The way mom sat tight-jawed in her chair it was if she was smug; like nothing was going to happen to her. After that, Mom got to speak and her words were so much less than genuine. She flippantly stated that "if" she had ever hurt her kids she didn't mean it and she was sorry. But it appeared as if her response were a canned response, without feeling or truth. It appeared she was telling the judge what he wanted to hear. Then Dad's lawyer spoke. She said she was in a most precarious position with a husband to her left and a wife to her right. The mother was hated and the father was loved. She toed the line and stated that dad instructed her that in no uncertain terms was she not to be antagonistic or say anything bad about the kids. No one was requesting hard time for dad and she requested that if he did get jail it would be work release jail. Then dad spoke. I cannot wait to get a copy of the transcripts to get his words exactly. He spoke of his parents and the good example they set, he apologized to his children through tears and you could tell his heart was broken. Then he talked to me. He told me he loved me and that the time we hugged in children's court was genuine and real and the only time we hugged in decades. His face was lowered and red with tears as he spoke. The pews behind the State were filled with his children in tears. I cannot tell you if it was the truth, but it felt genuine and I was so very, very grateful to hear those words from my father. I miss him and I will always miss him.

Then the judge said his piece. First, He sentenced dad who had already served nearly a year in jail with work release. He said he was confident of dad's partial responsibility but that he saw dad himself as somewhat of a victim. He talked about Dad's role and how he should have changed things. Dad was sentenced to a total of 20 months work release and with time served and good time credit. Because of his compliance without incident over the last year, he would only have to serve three more months and his term would be done. He won't be able to talk with his minor children unless one of us older siblings other than Lisa and Ricky supervise per the judge's order. He will have three years of probation and then he is done with his punishment. He can have no contact to any of the older children unless they want to and on their terms. That put a lot of minds at ease.

Then he sentenced mom. He admonished her for her 35 years of manipulation and stated that she was brilliant in her schemes and manipulations. He stated that prison can either be a punishment or to protect society. Judge Dreyfuss stated that he didn't feel she was threatening society, but the threat she posed to her own children was too great not to recognize. The judge referenced my statement several times. He stated, "Jennifer suggested that you get 35 years for the abuse you inflicted" and referenced many of the childrens' concerns from their statements. He described in his judgment how we were all united in our feelings for our mother and would address those concerns. Judge Dreyfuss sentenced her to three years in prison with no possibility of getting out early and then eight years of extended supervision and probation. During those eight years she would have to get a full-time job (which she has never had) and pay back the people she has stolen from. She will not be allowed to have a credit/debit card, credit/debit card numbers, a computer, internet access or checking accounts due to the extent of her fraud and financial crimes. The Judge stated that she was to have no contact with the minor children ever via any means until they reach the age of 18 (the youngest is now 13). She was instructed to have absolutely no contact with the adult children in any fashion or form unless they wanted that contact and requested it and on their terms. This is so important to all of us who want nothing to do with her.

Chapter 9

Child Abuse Prevention and my charity of choice, the Child Abuse Prevention Fund

The Child Abuse Prevention Fund is a special fund-raising initiative of Children's Hospital and Health System. Since 1988, the organization has distributed more than $6.7 million to support community-based prevention initiatives throughout Wisconsin. I began my association with this group a few years ago when I began to share our story for local fund-raising events. The more I became involved, the more I was moved by the efforts they support.

Children's Hospital and Health System is only too aware of the damage caused by child abuse and neglect, and the organization is working on many fronts to help end it. The health system's approach is two-pronged:

- To provide the medical care and resources necessary to help victims recover.
- To provide and seek support for primary prevention initiatives that stop abuse from happening in the first place.

All donations to the Child Abuse Prevention Fund help children and families across Wisconsin. Programs that can benefit from gifts include home visitation initiatives that help at-risk parents get started on the right foot when a new child is born; parent education programs that help parents be better parents; community education programs that deliver messages such as never shake a baby; and new, innovative approaches to strengthen families, enhance parenting skills and keep children safe from abuse and neglect.

Mission

The Child Abuse Prevention Fund is committed to ensuring a safe environment for children through financial support of primary prevention activities throughout Wisconsin, as well as educating professionals and the public about the role of prevention in eliminating child abuse.

History

In 1987, Milwaukee Brewers President Bud Selig, Milwaukee County Supervisor Thomas Bailey, and Children's Hospital and Health System President and CEO Jon E. Vice created the Child Abuse Prevention Fund to help combat the growing number of child abuse cases.

From the start, the Child Abuse Prevention Fund has recognized that the only true way to wipe out child abuse is through primary prevention - keeping child abuse from happening in the first place.

We as a community need everyone's help to stop child abuse and neglect

Child abuse and neglect are terrible problems. No child should have to grow up scared and hurt. Certainly, no child should die at the hands of a parent, family member or caregiver.

That's why societies help is so important. Thanks to the support of generous individuals, community groups and businesses, the Child Abuse Prevention Fund has provided more than $5 million for child abuse prevention programming throughout Wisconsin.

Prevalence of Child Abuse

It is difficult to determine exactly how many children are abused and neglected each year. Several state and national studies have been conducted, but because of the way the data was collected the results can be misleading and may not present an entirely accurate picture. For instance, we know that most research is based on cases of child abuse and neglect that have been substantiated by child protective services agencies, agencies which, due to their limited resources, are usually only able intervene in cases deemed to be of serious concern. We also know that many cases of abuse and neglect are never even reported. However, the most current data report that:

- In 2002, over three million reports of child abuse and neglect were made in the U.S. Approximately 896,000 children were found to have been victims of abuse or neglect.
- 3 children die in the United States each day from abuse or neglect.
- In 2003 in Wisconsin there were:
    o 40,473 reports of child abuse
    o 1,336 substantiated cases of physical abuse
    o 4,076 substantiated cases of sexual abuse
    o 36 substantiated cases of emotional abuse
    o 2,546 substantiated cases of child neglect
    o 12 substantiated cases of a child having died because of child abuse or neglect

Regardless of what the data says, we believe that one case of child abuse is one case too many.

Annual Report to the Governor and Legislature on Wisconsin Child Abuse and Neglect. Wisconsin Statutes, Section 48.981, Annual Report (Reporting Data for Calendar Year 2003) Office of Policy, Evaluation and Planning; Division of Children and Family Services, Department of Health and Family Services. www.dhfs.wisconsin.gov/cwreview/reports.htm

Contributing Factors to Child Abuse and Neglect

There is generally not a single factor that results in the abuse or neglect of a child; it is usually a combination of various factors. In addition, the duration (such as the duration of an illness) or intensity (such as the level of drug or alcohol abuse) can make it more or less likely that a child will be at risk for abuse. When trying to understand child abuse and neglect, we often look at possible factors in the adult, factors based on something in society, and factors based on something about the child.

Possible adult contributing factors

Research tells us that there is no "typical" abuser. People who abuse children may be male or female and the majority of child abuse is committed by someone who knows the child. In over 80% of cases a parent is the identified perpetrator. The following are characteristics of some people who abuse children.

- Low self-esteem
- Poor control over their emotions
- A history of being abused themselves
- Stress
- Financial problems
- Social isolation

- Relationship problems with a partner (may include domestic violence)
- Lack of parenting skills
- Is abusing drugs or alcohol
- Illness
- Belief that too much praise or attention will spoil a child
- Belief that fear and embarrassment are the way to make sure children obey
- Doesn't understand children's needs or abilities and criticizes children who can't meet their high expectations
- Belief that children should be quiet at all times
- Inability to cope with life stressors
- Focused on own troubles or things other than their children
- Has been diagnosed or exhibits symptoms of depression

Possible societal contributing factors

There are many deeply rooted, complicated and interrelated societal factors that can contribute to child abuse and neglect. While we cannot list them all here, the following two factors are often identified as increasing the likelihood that child abuse and neglect will occur.

- Stresses of poverty
- Community violence

Possible child contributing factors

Some children have certain characteristics or behaviors that make it more likely that they will be at risk for abuse or neglect. However, it is important to remember that no matter what characteristics a child has or how they act a child is NEVER responsible for being abused or neglected.

- Illness, especially chronic illness
- Disability
- Crying for extended periods
- Feeding problems
- Tantrums and whining
- Biting
- Toilet learning
- Disobedience and lying
- Physical appearance (for example, resembles someone who is viewed negatively by the caregiver)
- Poor grades

Correlations

Child Abuse, Neglect and Domestic Violence

- There is a significant overlap between abuse of women and children. One study estimated that 30-40 percent of women who are abused have children who are abused.
- Domestic violence is the single major precursor to child deaths in the U.S. It is estimated that 70% of cases in which an abused child dies, their mother has been the victim of domestic violence.
- It is believed that child abuse is 15 times more likely when there is domestic violence in the home.
- When child abuse is substantiated, 42% of those children lived in homes where there was domestic violence.

- Living in an abusive home puts children in greater risk of being hurt as they may:
  - be the target of displaced anger or frustration of either parent - abused mothers are 8 times more likely to abuse children when they are battered than when they are safe
  - try to protect their parent and in the process be injured
  - be hurt accidentally if they get in the way

Children who grow up in a violent home tend to experience:

- Danger
- Fear and tension
- Chaos
- Confusion
- Isolation
- Helplessness
- A love/hate relationship with their parents

Effects of Domestic Violence on Children

- Children who witness domestic violence at home display emotional and behavioral disturbances such as withdrawal, low self-esteem, nightmares, self-blame and aggression towards peers, family members and property.
- 30% of children who witness domestic violence go on to become perpetrators of violence compared to 2-4% of people in the general population.
- When boys are exposed to severe domestic violence they are ten times more likely as adults to be violent towards their partner.

Child Abuse/Neglect and Alcoholism/Drug Abuse

- Alcohol and other drug abuse affects children both emotionally and physically. In their pre-occupation with alcohol, parents may neglect their children's needs.
- Children's self-esteem may suffer as parents might call them names or embarrass them in front of others.
- Children may feel frustrated, unhappy, confused, angry, frightened, ashamed.

Children affected by adult's problems with alcohol or drugs may be:

- insecure and have related behavior problems like delinquency, aggression, passiveness.
- overly responsible and take on tasks their parents or caretakers would normally do, such as feeding themselves and caring for younger siblings.
- unable to trust others and express feelings.

Possible contributing factors to abuse/neglect by someone abusing alcohol/drugs include:

- The drinking parent "losing control" and using alcohol as an excuse.
- The non-drinking parent taking his or her resentment of the drinking parent out on the child.
- Either parent having unrealistic ideas about what to expect from a child at a certain age.
- Alcohol lowers a person's inhibitions and so they may take risks and make decisions that could harm

someone. The use of alcohol is often linked with incidents of child sexual abuse.

- Caretakers who drink may neglect their child because they are too involved with alcohol to be aware of the child. A non-drinking parent may be too burdened by his or her spouse's demands to care for the child.

Child Abuse, Neglect and Poverty

Families who live in poverty are subject to constant stress. Poverty is often accompanied by the stress of unemployment and inadequate housing. In addition, there may be other problems such as mental illness and substance abuse. Living in poverty puts children at greater risk for maltreatment as they live under these stressful and often unsafe conditions. Parents may lose hope and lack the energy to overcome any additional stress. To cope with their stress parents may withdraw or lash out at their children.

The Third National Incidence Study of Child Abuse and Neglect found that children from families with annual incomes below $15,000 were over 22 times more likely to experience maltreatment than children from families whose incomes exceeded $30,000. These children were also 18 times more likely to be sexually abused, almost 56 times more likely to be educationally neglected, and over 22 times more likely to be seriously injured.

Other research has found that young children living in poverty are more likely to be born at a low birth weight, receive lower quality medical care, experience hunger and malnutrition, experience high levels of interpersonal conflict in their homes, and be exposed to violence and environmental toxins in their neighborhoods, all of which place children at greater risk for maltreatment or harm. In addition, research has found that children who live in poverty are more likely to: experience delays in their physical, cognitive, language, and emotional development which, in turn, affect their readiness for school; be hospitalized during childhood; and die in infancy or early childhood.

Costs of Child Abuse & the Need for More Prevention

- Three children die each day from abuse or neglect- a cost that is incalculable.
- Abuse takes an enormous toll on children, both physically and emotionally.
- Child abuse causes a drain on social, health and judicial services.
- Adults who were abused or neglected as children are more likely to go on to commit crimes.
- Child abuse costs taxpayers $258 million each day and $94 billion a year.
- A conservative estimate is that child abuse costs each family $1,400 a year.
- Only $1.06 per family is spent each year for programs to prevent child abuse.

(Information from Prevent Child Abuse America)

Costs of Child Abuse and Neglect in Wisconsin

According to a 2002 cost-analysis released by the Wisconsin Children's Trust Fund, child abuse and neglect costs Wisconsin more than $789 million a year or $2.16 million a day. That is 98 times more than the $8.07 million that is spent to protect Wisconsin children from abuse and neglect. Using conservative estimates, and without accounting for the incalculable cost of the loss of 17 Wisconsin children's lives (2001), the Children's Trust Fund reported the following staggering direct and indirect costs of abuse.

Direct Costs (costs associated with the immediate needs of abused or neglected children):

Estimated Annual Cost

Hospitalization: $12.9 million
Chronic Health Problems: $20.6 million
Mental Health Care System: $13.8 million
Child Welfare Services: $452.0 million
Law Enforcement: $0.3 million
Judicial System: $2.2 million

Total Direct Costs $501.8 million

Indirect Costs (costs associated with the long-term care or secondary effects of child abuse and neglect):

Estimated Annual Cost

Special Education: $5.8 million
Mental Health and Health Care: $1.7 million
Juvenile Delinquency: $26.2 million
Lost Productivity to Society: $60.6 million
Adult Criminality: $100.1 million

Total Indirect Costs $287.2 million

TOTAL COST child abuse/neglect in WI **$789 million**

Escape from the Dungeon

For more information and descriptions of the rationales used to determine each cost area, go to: http://wctf.state.wi.us.

With help, we can stop child abuse and neglect as a community.....

CAP Fund's vision for the future is one where all children are loved, cared for and nurtured. Sadly, we as society are a long way from that vision. Every year in Wisconsin alone, there are more than 40,000 reports of child abuse and neglect.

The support of the Child Abuse Prevention Fund goes a long way toward making their vision a reality. Gifts of time, talent and financial resources support programs throughout Wisconsin that help parents be better parents with the result: more children living without the threat of physical, verbal and emotional abuse.

Here in the state of Wisconsin, a State Call to Action to end child abuse and neglect began April 29, 2004 at a summit convened by Governor Jim Doyle in Madison, Wisconsin. The Governor's Summit to Prevent Child Abuse and Neglect was video-taped for an archived web cast that took the Call to Action statewide.

The Child Abuse Prevention Fund was a sponsor the Governor's Summit and is coordinating the State Call to Action to end child abuse and neglect in Wisconsin.

The State Call to Action initiative will mobilize people concerned about the well-being of Wisconsin's children to work together toward the following goals:

- Raise awareness of the human and economic costs of child abuse and neglect.
- Propose short- and long-term child abuse and neglect prevention strategies.
- Strengthen public will, resources and community capacity to prevent child abuse and neglect.

Below are some tips and actions provided by the Child Abuse Prevention Fund that can assist you in the difficult task of parenting:

Parenting Tips

Being a parent can be the most rewarding experience in life. But as many parents know, raising a child is not always easy. As human beings, we can't always control events in our life or how we feel. But as adults and parents, we must always be in control of how we treat children. Following are tips and guidelines parents can use to develop their own positive approach to parenting:

"As a parent, I promise to..."

- Show my children daily that I love them by what I say and do.
- At least once a day praise something about my children; be wary of excessive criticism.
- Give my children freedom and privacy and teach them the proper use of both.
- Keep my house suitable for children's activities, and a welcome place for their friends.
- Do these activities with my children: read a book, go to a picnic, and visit friends.
- Be extra careful before I speak when I am tired.

- Recognize and respect my children's individualism and do not expect them to be the same.
- Keep promises I make to my children and teach them to be dependable.
- Say, "I love you."

Information submitted to Metropolitan Missionary Baptist Church, Rev. Willie D. Wanzo, Sr., author unknown

Words that help

A child with self-esteem will have the confidence to succeed. Use words that validate your child's feelings and give him or her encouragement, such as:

- "I/We love you."
- "Good job."
- "I'm/We're so proud of you."
- "We can do it together."
- "Thanks for your help."
- "What did you like best about today?"

Words that hurt

Words can make a child feel worthless, ugly and unloved. Children believe what their parents tell them, and can be hurt by such phrases as:

- "Stupid! You never do anything right."
- "You're more trouble than you're worth."
- "I'm sick of you! Why don't you find another place to live?"
- "You're so lazy. You'll never amount to anything."
- "Why can't you be as smart as your brother? He always gets A's."

Actions that help

- It's important to make sure your children know they can always come to you when they feel confused, afraid or threatened.
- Keep the line of communication open and take time to LISTEN to your children.
- Believe a child who tells you about sexual abuse. Tell the child you know it's not the child's fault. Promise to get help.
- Here's some advice to give your children: If you are abused or if someone threatens to abuse you, tell someone about it.
- Abusers say a child's threat to tell someone about abuse is the best way to keep abuse from ever happening.

What is child abuse?
Child abuse or neglect includes:

- Physical abuse or neglect
- Emotional abuse (words that hurt) or neglect
- Leaving a child unsupervised
- Sexual abuse
- Abandonment
- Educational neglect

By associating ourselves with organizations like the CAP Fund we as society can bind together to change the course for those that are abused or who are recovering from abuse. There are so many organizations out there but I must say that I have been endeared to this one for their tireless efforts year after year and would encourage support on their behalf.

Signs of Child Abuse and Neglect

Abuse and neglect may show up in physical or behavioral signs, some of which are listed here. In many instances there appears to be an unusual pattern or location of physical injuries that suggests abuse. Some of the signs listed may indicate problems that do not involve abuse or neglect. If you suspect abuse, report it to the appropriate local agency and let them make the determination.

Children's Physical Signs:

o   Bruises, welts or broken bones
o   Burns
o   Missing hair
o   Poor hygiene
o   Injuries or redness around the genitals
o   Injuries at different stages of healing
o   Injury or medical condition that hasn't been properly treated
o   Slowed physical development

Children's Behavioral Signs:

o   poor grades
o   lack of concentration
o   frequent tardiness or absence from school
o   difficulty making and keeping friends
o   unhappiness, depression
o   withdrawal from others
o   acts of anger, aggression
o   destruction of property

o hurting themselves or others
o low self-esteem
o problems with expressing feelings
o fatigue
o constant attention seeking
o speech problems
o sleeping problems
o reluctance to go home
o hunger, begging for food, stealing
o unusual fears
o unusual knowledge of sex

Chapter 10

How the kids are doing today

1988-2005 - Jennifer's life after the storm – Well, now that you have read everything, I hope you can understand why I am so thankful for the accomplishments I have been graced by God to complete since I turned 18. It wasn't all easy just because I was able to escape the dungeon. In 1991 when my mother called her press conference to have that story published to say nothing had ever happened, I hit rock bottom once again. She had escaped all charges, she has escaped all accountability for her actions. All the children who were still under the age 18 were returned to the home. This woman would see no retribution for her actions. I was devastated and distraught and then somehow, someway, I walked into an Army recruiter's office. I don't know what took me there but it is a day I will never regret. I had 60 credits of college and was 21 years old. I joined the Reserves and worked at 84th Division on Silver Spring Drive in Milwaukee. I attended basic training and laughed the whole time: I got my own bunk, a locker and all the food I could eat, I was in heaven. I smiled a little bit when the drill sergeants said they were going to break us down and then build us up. They said this would be the most miserable 9 weeks of my life -- I smiled because I knew it wouldn't be. I found a home for the first time in 21 years. I trained hard, really hard, and every time the drill sergeants yelled at me while I was doing push ups all I kept thinking was "Is that all you got?". I loved my training and then I met a wonderful man who I fell in love with and dated for three years. I moved to South Carolina and went to a college there to be closer to him. After High School, Meg and I touched base off and on through the years and then she wrote me a letter with her telephone number. I thought she wrote it wrong because it was the same area code as mine. Low and behold if wonders would never cease, Meg was going to graduate school in Columbia, SC, the very same town where I was living! I think we were both floored to discover we had ended up in the same town halfway across the country and didn't even know it. I think it is too weird to be a coincidence and I really believe there is a higher power working in my life. We spent the next few months getting to be friends again and going out and having a good time like normal college students. Meg eventually moved on to Germany to work for a big international company and I followed the love of my life to his next duty assignment. He was the first man on earth I truly trusted and told all of my stories to. He was the first man that I loved. He was everything I looked for and he could do no wrong in my eyes. After three years I wanted to make a better life for us so I went active duty and went to Officer Candidate School in June 1994 to become a 2nd Lieutenant in the Army. This was the toughest training under the toughest conditions. There were only 13 women in my class of 273 and the odds were stacked against me. I had a ranger and a Special Forces soldier in my squad and they did not like women. For 14 ½ weeks those guys tried to get me to quit. We walked through swamps, dug eight foxholes in seven days with full overhead cover and we went on reconnaissance missions. They made me carry the M60 with no strap and the radio every mission (this was heavy as a side note). We had to do ranger pushups with our feet elevated on trees behind us and we faced tough, tough conditions. I wanted to quit 50 times, but I gutted through. After training I met up with the love of my life before proceeding to my Officer Basic Course at Fort Eustis, VA. While in my class I found out I was pregnant. I remember calling my love on the phone and trying to look at the pink stick through my tears. He said the baby wasn't his – and he left me with the tears and all. Life had sent me another blow. I cried for months and months and I tried to convince him over and over that he needed to be

Jennifer M. Stephens

there for me. Around the 5th month of pregnancy when I
moved to my permanent duty station of Fort Knox, KY, I
realized that I only had one person to depend on, and that
was me. I remember moving myself into my home on
post, carrying furniture and a TV into the house while 5
months pregnant. I didn't know anyone – I didn't trust
anyone. The neighbor down the street took pity on me
and helped me move the rest into the house. I remember
lying on my couch night after night crying to my unborn
child; I will never hurt you, I will never, ever hurt you. I
will work for you harder than I would ever work for
myself. When the time came and I was in labor, I had to
drive myself to the hospital because I just didn't know
anyone. My aunt, who was my suedo mother for years
after I left home in 1987, came down to Kentucky for the
first week to help me with the new baby. I am so grateful
for her.

When I had my daughter Samantha, that was the
day my world changed for the rest of my life. The Friday
before I went into labor I was in school, I had my
daughter on Saturday and on Monday she went to school
with me as I sat on a pillow in my Spanish class. Sam went
with me every day and I got a 4.0 semester. For the next
two years I worked all day and took Sam to school with
me at night. I got my two undergraduate degrees when
she was two and, because I had no one to watch her while
I went through the graduation ceremony, she went with
me and walked across the stage. My professors gave her
the degree for her sacrifices. I spent the next few years
getting a MBA and doing wonderful things for the military
and was even the boat commander in Pearl Harbor,
Hawaii before moving back home to Wisconsin for a tour
of duty.

I didn't date after Sam was born, I just lost trust in
men after that incident, but in 2002 I met someone. He

was a major in the Army and I thought he was the one. I fell for him instantly and thought he and I would be together forever. We even talked about him being a step dad to my daughter; I considered it. He was the first man I ever introduced to my daughter and then, yes, I got pregnant. Much like the first pregnancy, as I cried looking at the stick and called him on the phone, he said it wasn't his and he wanted proof and he couldn't come see me because he was going to his other girlfriend's house. As you can imagine, that did not turn out well and is an issue I deal with to this day. However, good came out of it and I have a son named Blakely Thomas Raymond after my dad and my grandfather. He is simply a momma's boy and I live to please him on a daily basis. I look at my two children and thank God daily for them. Sometimes when I allow myself to reflect, I simply wonder how a mother could hurt her child. The worst thing that could have happened to my mother was for me to have kids, because everyday when I tell them I love them and hug them and kiss them, it renews my strength to help my brothers and sisters who cannot fight for themselves.

I have enrolled in law school now and hope to get my degree so that after I retire from the military I can continue to help those who cannot fight for themselves -- but we will see how the bar exams go before I make plans for the future. I also hope to run for Congress or State Senate in Wisconsin one day so I can initiate change in our system. Right now, I wish I were three people to accomplish all that I want to accomplish, but all I got is time and the drive to achieve it all. Meg's mom laughs at me every time we talk because she knows I have these big ideas about how I am going to change the world. I must say that I wouldn't trade the way I grew up for the world because that is what made me the way I am today, and I am happy with the person I am right now.

Does my story have a happy end? I certainly hope so. I continue in my daily struggles with trials and tribulations just as anyone does. I am pregnant with my third child and finishing my law degree. I love my kids and I love my job – what more could a person want besides winning the lottery.

Jennifer's military biography:

MAJOR Jennifer Stephens entered the military as a PFC in September 1991. Her enlisted assignments include 84th Div (TNG) in Milwaukee, WI, 108th Div (TNG), in Charlotte, NC, 482nd Eng Plt (Firefighters) at Fort Riley, KS and the 369th Signal Battalion at Fort Gordon, GA.

After being promoted to Sergeant in 1994 she went to Officer Candidate School at Fort Benning, GA where she was commissioned as a 2nd Lieutenant in the Transportation Corps. She then attended the Transportation Officer Basic Course at Fort Eustis, VA after which she was assigned to the 16th Cavalry Regiment at Fort Knox, KY. There she was the operations officer for the International Military Student Office supporting officers from over 50 different countries. She then went to the 1st Armor Training Brigade where she was an Executive Officer in A/3-81 Armor Battalion.

In 1998 she completed the Combined Logistics Officer Advanced Course (CLOAC) at Fort Lee, VA and the Combined Arms and Services School (CAS3) at Fort Leavenworth, KS. In November 1998 MAJ Stephens went to Schofield Barracks where she served as the Adjutant for the 524th Corps Support Battalion in the 45th Corps Support Group (Forward) through May of 2000 supporting 600 troops. She then served as the 545th Transportation (Harbormaster) company commander where she had three detachments assigned to her: 545th Harbormaster, 605th Transportation Logistic Support

Vessel (LSV 2) and the 193rd Transportation (LSV 5). She worked with 19 CW3's and 100 enlisted personnel and was responsible for all Army LSV operations in the Pacific Theater.

MAJ Stephens then worked as a Active Component/Reserve Component (AC/RC) liaison with the 336th Transportation Group at Fort Sheridan, Illinois where she spearheaded the USARC exercise Nationwide Move '02 transporting troops and equipment spanning 18 states and over 1,000,000 miles and she earned the Army Transportation Officer of the Year award. She then moved to another AC/RC assignment with the 3-335th Training Support Battalion where she worked with 129 units in the state of Illinois and was responsible for training for over 6000 mobilizing reservists and national guard members for Operation Iraqi Freedom and Operation Enduring Freedom.

Currently MAJ Stephens is working as an Assistant Professor of Military Science and Officer in Charge at the University of Wisconsin- Whitewater. She has Bachelor's Degree in International Business and Finance from the University of Louisville, KY, and a Masters in Business Administration and Global Management from the University of Phoenix, AZ. MAJ Stephens is also currently in the Concord School of Law earning her Juris Doctor degree.

Her awards and decorations include the Army Transportation Officer of the Year Award 2002, Meritorious Service Medal, Army Commendation Medal (3rd award), Army Achievement Medal, National Defense Service Ribbon (2nd Award), Overseas Ribbon, Global War on Terrorism Award, and the Army Service Ribbon.

Below is a description of how the remaining 15 kids are doing today:

Ted: Ted has been very successful in his life due to good old fashion hard work. After we left home he and I spent a lot of time with our grandpa Stephens and he guided Ted in proper financial management, business management and many other life lessons. Ted now owns his own trucking fleet and his own business with his wife and three children. His wife has probably been the one greatest factor in his happiness. I couldn't imagine a better suited pair.

Jennifer: As stated in my bio, I am a single mom with two kids. Every day I struggle with how to discipline my children, but every single day I know I will never hit them. My daughter knows if I lose my temper that she has to walk away and spend some time in her room in order for me to cool off. I am very open with my kids about how I grew up, because I want each generation to get better and better and the only way to do that is to communicate. I hope to finish my 20 years in the military and then either work in a private family law practice or in Waukesha County. I would also like to run for congress in some fashion simply to help children and because there are too few veterans making decisions for the men and women in uniform and I would like to change that.

Holly: Holly is raising a wonderful family and is very in love with her husband. She also works on her accounting degree during the day when the kids are at school. She has found peace and solace and enjoys the life she has made for herself and her family.

Elizabeth: Elizabeth is an extremely successful real estate agent who works out of her home with her husband and is expecting her third child as I write this. She has an incredible amount of drive simply unparalleled by her peers.

Chip: Chip has had a few rough spots with jobs and relationships but continues to take steps forward every day.

Roger: Roger has three children and is very dedicated to them and works full time to support them.

Ricky: Ricky has had several incidents with the law and drug use. I cannot state at this time if he is working or if he still uses drugs. He supports mom 100% and I cannot offer good reasons for that.

Suzy: Suzy has had a troubled few years since she turned 18 and is still trying to find herself. She too has had issues with drug and alcohol but attempts to grab a hold of those issues on a daily basis. She is currently engaged to someone she met in a recovery program but both still fight the addictions while they are starting a family together. I hope Suzy finds herself and the path she is destined to take.

Michael: Michael is completing his senior year at UW-Milwaukee and intends to go to grad school to be a chiropractor. He works very hard and is very dedicated to improving his lifestyle. Michael is exactly one of the reasons I am writing this book. I would absolutely love to go up to him one day and give him a check for his college tuition and books and go to his graduation.

Andie: Andie is graduating Marquette University in December 2005 and will be going to Medical School hopefully in Chicago. She has met a wonderful fellow who supports her unconditionally. They have been dating for years and I will be happy to attend their wedding in the not too distant future (hint, hint Paul). Andie too has an unquenchable thirst to succeed and continually wants to help her brothers and sisters. It would make me smile to help her with medical school so she can start out on the best foot possible and take care of others.

Lisa: Lisa continues to support mom in her endeavors and is quite emotional at every court hearing. She seems incredibly frail and she deals with diabetes on a daily basis. I hope she finds success on her own so she can begin the healing process.

Mary: Mary is currently a PFC in the Marine Corps and stationed in Japan. She goes to college in her off-duty time and is making the most out of her adventure. She misses her family terribly but realizes the benefits she is receiving right now are the best thing for her. I think she went into the Marines because Ted was in the Navy and I am in the Army and she wanted to do her own thing... I do remind her though that she will always have to salute me (chuckle, chuckle).

Jeffery: I had custody of Jeffery for a while and he has come such a long way in the last year. He graduated from high school and has moved into his own apartment. He works full-time at Home Depot (mega mart hardware store) and is excited about having health care as a full-time employee. Jeffery also started a side business doing odd jobs for neighbors around the neighborhood and is starting to build a client base. He is on the right track and I hope it continues.

Nick: Nick also came to live with me shortly after he was removed from the house and went through a traumatic transition much like the oldest kids went through 18 years ago. He had never met me before and then all of a sudden I had temporary custody. He moved in with me and often shut down. He then spent time with Ted, my older brother, and finally went to a permanent foster home where he is thriving. Nick is going to be a senior next year and seems to grasp the idea of hard work paying off. He gets good grades and he works on side jobs and is always lending a hand to me whenever he can. He is so good with my son and shows great parental instincts and is very caring by nature. I am confident he will be a good father when the day comes..... far in the future.

Charlie: Charlie is thriving in his foster home. He has Type I diabetes and has learned to manage his condition, which is a huge feat in itself. He has some behavior issues, most of which can be attributed to being a 14 year old boy, but it is a struggle none the less. Charlie has repeatedly stated his desire to remain in his foster home until he turns 18 so he doesn't have to go home.

Amber: Amber is thriving in her foster home as well. I had custody of her too for a short time but her foster home is able to give her the attention that I cannot as a single mother too close to the situation. She gets great grades, hangs out with friends and spends time at my house and sometimes goes with me to my work functions in the military. She even rode with me in a Memorial Day parade! Amber said she wants to join the military and get stationed with me and my sister Mary in the Marines... I will support her 100% in this endeavor.

In general, we all have struggles and successes much like any other person living in this world. Some of the kids have dealt with our history better than others. Even the ones who are dealing with it well like myself, have momentary lapses of reason that force us to refocus in order to live a healthy full life. As the oldest daughter, the suedo matriarch of the family, there is one thing I want all of my brothers and sisters to know, I want them to know how proud I am of their accomplishments and ability to overcome obstacles. We are survivors who have and will continue to succeed in a wide variety of fields and will continue to defy statistics. We older children live to set the example for the younger children. We try to show success in spite of circumstance and to never rely on anything less than your hard work to get where you want to go. Not one of the children has resorted to the abuse our mother bestowed onto us throughout our lives and we all continually seek to better ourselves and our families… despite the way mom raised us.

Chapter 11

Photos

Jennifer M. Stephens

Escape from the Dungeon

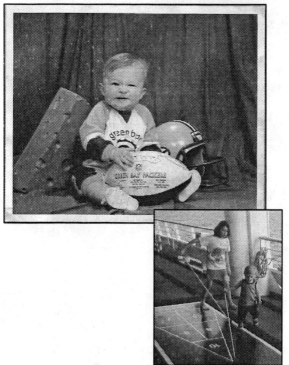

Escape from the Dungeon

Sources of information:

1. Court records pertaining to #87-CF-517, #87-CF-516 (1987 child abuse allegations)
2. Court records pertaining to #PR04-08879, #PR04-008878, PR04-08834, PR04-08833, PR04-08619 04CF1063, PR04-06691, PR04-06690 (2004 child abuse allegations)
3. Reports of the New Berlin Police Department
4. Letters from Linda Stephens to outside sources to include: judges, grandparents, siblings, and the media
5. My own personal memories and recollections
6. Public records on Wisconsin Circuit Court Access Program
7. *http://www.kathleen-sullivan.com/Stockholm%20Syndrome.htm*
8. *http://www.mental-health-Michaelers.com/articles¹/article.php?artID=469*

ISBN 141206579-8

9 781412 065795